Reflective Project

Skills for Success

HODDER
EDUCATION
AN HACHETTE UK COMPANY

FOR THE
IB CP

Reflective Project

Skills for Success

Rebecca Austin Pickard

HODDER
EDUCATION
AN HACHETTE UK COMPANY

Orders: please contact Bookpoint Ltd, 130 Park Drive, Milton Park, Abingdon, Oxon OX14 4SE. Telephone: (44) 01235 827827. Fax: (44) 01235 400401. Email education@bookpoint.co.uk Lines are open from 9 a.m. to 5 p.m., Monday to Saturday, with a 24-hour message answering service. You can also order through our website: www.hoddereducation.com

ISBN: 978 1 5104 7136 8

© Rebecca Austin Pickard 2019

First published in 2019 by
Hodder Education,
An Hachette UK Company
Carmelite House
50 Victoria Embankment
London EC4Y 0DZ

www.hoddereducation.com

Impression number 10 9 8 7 6 5 4 3 2 1

Year   2023 2022 2021 2020 2019

Cover photo © storm – stock.adobe.com

Illustrations by Aptara Inc.

Typeset in India by Aptara Inc.

Printed in Spain

A catalogue record for this title is available from the British Library.

Contents

Introduction

How to use this book

Welcome to Reflective Project for the IB Career related Programme: Skills for Success.

This guide will help you prepare for the reflective project systematically, building your skills every step of the way. Each chapter of the book looks at a different aspect of the reflective project in detail, while practice exercises are also included to help you check your understanding.

To ensure students benefit most from the reflective project, there is an emphasis from the start on the *process* rather than just the *product*. However, every stage is designed so students can aim for the best grade for them. This guide:

- Includes an opening infographic spread in each chapter

- Builds skills for success through a range of reflective, ethical and critical thinking strategies and expert advice such as creating research questions and carrying out research correctly

- Covers all the IB requirements with clear breakdowns of the assessment criteria and rules of academic honesty

- Adds reference to the IB Learner Profile

Key features of the guide include:

LEARNER PROFILE ATTRIBUTES

Learner profile attributes are highlighted at the start of chapters 1–3 and 5–11.

EXPERT TIP

These tips appear throughout the book and provide guidance on steps you can take and key things you should consider in order to help boost your final grade.

COMMON MISTAKE

Potential pitfalls are highlighted for students in the form of 'Common mistakes'. Watch out for these!

EXAMPLE TASK

In some chapters short tasks are included. These tasks give you the opportunity to apply the knowledge of the chapter in example situations.

REFLECTION POINT

These boxes offer opportunities to review aspects of the reflective project you have worked on so far. It is important to reflect on your progress so look out for these!

CHAPTER SUMMARY KEY POINTS

At the end of each chapter key knowledge is distilled in to a short checklist to help you review everything you have learned over the previous pages.

Throughout the book, activities are divided into three categories:

- Thinking
- Doing
- Reflecting

Each of these can be identified by the following icons:

THINKING

Thinking activities require students to consider some of the key ideas of the course or respond to source material, and to share their thoughts with their classmates.

DOING

Doing activities prompt students to carry out an investigation, discover and communicate ideas and information, or perform a practical application of their learning.

REFLECTING

Reflecting activities ask students to think deeply about their own skills, qualities and practices. They often recommend students record their thoughts in a journal, blog or other media.

About the author

Rebecca Austin Pickard is an experienced IB educator working extensively across both the CP and DP programmes. She was IBCP coordinator at Dane Court Grammar School in Broadstairs, Kent, UK until 2017 and supported many other schools in Kent establishing the CP. She is currently a CP Consultant for the IB, working with schools in the AEM region as well as a IB Workshop Leader. She is also in the final stages of completing a MA in English and American Literature at the University of Kent, Canterbury in the UK.

Where does the Reflective Projec

Theme	Links to reflective project
1 Personal development	Forms the basis for self-reflection and explores the skills required to organize and manage time, make decisions and manage change; students require all of these to complete the reflective project successfully.
2 Intercultural understanding	Directly links with students' need to develop an appreciation of how cultural contexts may affect different perspectives on an ethical dilemma.
3 Effective communication	Its focus on interpersonal communication, writing, presentation and IT skills strengthens students' ability to present a structured and coherent project.
4 Thinking processes	The topics of ethical thinking, critical thinking, creative thinking, problem-solving and lateral thinking have direct application to the ways in which students learn and engage with the reflective project.
5 Applied ethics	Allows students to explore ethics, develop understandings, examine case studies and identify a focus for their reflective project.

The reflective project will assess the following criteria, which are to be demonstrated throughout the reflective project process, from identification of an ethical dilemma embedded in an issue linked to your career-related study, to planning, through to reflection.

	Students will be expected to:
Criterion A: Focus and method	• select and explore an ethical dilemma embedded in an issue linked to a career-related context • select and apply appropriate research methods and collect and select relevant information from a variety of sources, showing an understanding of bias and validity
Criterion B: Knowledge and understanding in context	• demonstrate knowledge and understanding of the issue • contextualize the ethical dilemma and analyse different perspectives on it through the use of a local/global example of the issue in which the dilemma is embedded • demonstrate awareness and understanding of the impact of the ethical dilemma on a local/global community and the cultural influences on, and perceptions of, the ethical dilemma
Criterion C: Critical thinking	• demonstrate logical reasoning processes and the ability to interpret, analyse and evaluate material • develop the ability to synthesize information, making connections and linking ideas and evidence
Criterion D: Communication	• present a structured and coherent project, use appropriate terminology accurately and consistently and communicate ideas and concepts clearly
Criterion E: Engagement and reflections on planning and progress	• reflect on and refine the research process, and react to insights gained through exploration of the ethical dilemma • critique decisions made throughout the research process and suggest improvements to their own working practices

1 Understanding the Reflective Project objectives

Context of the Reflective Project

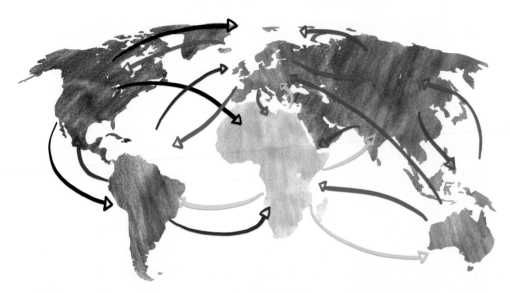

Why is ethical reflection important to the world and IBCP? What is the purpose of the reflective project?

The reflective project is a requirement for all CP students and gives you the opportunity to develop **intercultural understanding** as well as the opportunity to explore and **reflect** on the relevance of the IB Career-related Programme to your own life. It draws together all the important strands of the CP in one formal assessment that explores **cultural perspectives** on an **ethical dilemma** centred in your **career-related subject,** which allows you **to explore real-life situations**.

It is a project unique to each student and takes place over an extended period of time so you have the time to develop a wide range of ethical, analytical and reflective skills and will be able to demonstrate and reflect on your personal development. By investigating and reflecting on cultural values and behaviours, you will gain a greater understanding and respect for how others lead their lives.

ACTIVITY: HOW DOES CULTURE IMPACT PERSPECTIVES?

'Identifying how culture can impact perspectives on a day-to-day basis and developing new informed ideas is a powerful skill which can have a positive impact on your future and others.'

Think of negative stories in the local, national or international news and consider what role cultural misunderstanding, ignorance or miscommunication played.

ACTIVITY: WHAT ASPECTS OF CULTURE DO YOU THINK INFLUENCE OPINION?

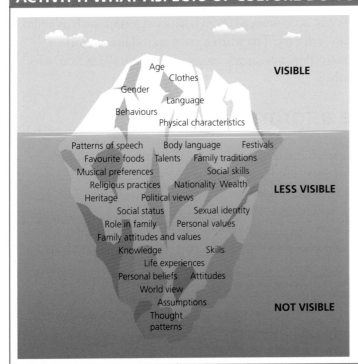

Look at the cultural iceberg image and notice the idea of three levels of visibility in terms of cultural influences.

With a partner, take turns to say the first opinions that come to mind with aspects of each of these levels you are drawn to. Then review where you had similarities and differences of opinion and why that might have been. What aspects of culture do you think influence your opinion?

The Reflective Project's aims

The reflective project is assessed on THE PROCESS as well as THE OUTPUT, which is why this book is designed to help you use your initiative and benefit from every step of the process and not just focus on the final piece.

In summary, through the reflective project, you will:

- produce an in-depth piece of work over a minimum of 50 hours

- engage in personal inquiry, action and reflection on a specific ethical dilemma

- present a structured and coherent argument

- engage with local and/or global communities

- develop high-level research, writing and communication skills

- develop the skills of critical and creative thinking

- submit your work to be marked by your school and externally moderated by the IB.

What format can the Reflective Project take?

■ Option 1

A written essay of no more than 3,000 words as well as the Reflections on planning and progress form (RPPF) of no more than 1,000 words. The essay should cover all the reflective project's requirements except Criterion E Reflection, which will be assessed by the RPPF only.

■ Option 2

A written essay (1,500–2,000 words) accompanied by an additional format such as a film, oral presentation, interview, play or display. The written essay and additional format should cover all the reflective project's requirements except Criterion E Reflection, which will be assessed by the RPPF only.

How do I choose a format?

Be open-minded and consider each format, as there are no easy options here. It can be tempting to say 'I'll just do an essay' but remember that you will be spending a lot of time on this project and you need to be honest about how you work best. This is an opportunity to develop skills creatively, and also a chance to consider how working in more than one format might suit you for a variety of reasons. Perhaps you are already familiar with the additional formats from your Diploma subjects or they might all be unfamiliar but you would like to try something new.

A benefit of the additional format is that it allows you to develop creatively an aspect of your reflective project that might not be possible in your accompanying essay. Look carefully at the additional format and extra information below before making a final decision.

■ Additional formats

A written essay (1,500–2,000 words) with an additional format of:

A short film	This can be any type of film such as a documentary, drama, news report (7 minutes) or you can submit a written film script of 700 words instead.	To see how powerfully and creatively a short film can communicate serious, ethical issues do some exploration. For example: **https://sites.google. com/a/b05ortuella.net/teaching-in-english/ ethics-and-ethical-values/short-films**
A spoken presentation	This can be recorded on audio/ video (7 minutes) or a written script of 700 words instead.	From TedTalks to podcasts, the spoken presentation is a very popular medium today. A chance to develop this skill is always valuable. What type of spoken presentations do you listen to yourself? What aspects most appeal to you?
An interview	Recorded on audio/video (7 minutes) or a written script of 700 words instead.	Budding journalist or not, this is an interesting option where you are invited to create an interview which requires imaginative inquiry and subject matter. Look at **https://blog.ted.com/black-lives- matter-storycorps-interviews/** for a good example of the importance of interviewing.
A play	Recorded on audio/video (7 minutes) or a written script of 700 words instead.	Perhaps drama is one of your passions and this format is great chance to develop your own work. Look at **www.bbc.co.uk/writersroom/ writers-lab** for more inspiration.
A display	A storyboard or photo essay using up to 15 annotated images; 700 words.	A storyboard/photo essay is usually a linear narrative told through imagery. What different impacts can be achieved through imagery? Get inspired by **www.worldpressphoto.org/** and **http://time.com/3687500/photojournalism- links-january/**

How is the Reflective Project assessed?

■ Assessment criteria at a glance

A: Focus and method	6 marks	■ Ethical dilemma and issue ■ Research question ■ Methodology
B: Knowledge and understanding in context	9 marks	■ Context ■ Local or global example ■ Alternative perspectives and perceptions of dilemma
C: Critical thinking	12 marks	■ Research ■ Analysis ■ Discussion and evaluation
D: Communication	3 marks	■ Structure ■ Layout
E: Engagement and reflection	6 marks	■ Process ■ Engagement ■ Research focus

Total marks: 36

ACTIVITY: REFLECTION

Which of these criteria have you explored already in your Core, CRS or DP subjects?

■ Assessment criteria in more detail

Students will be expected to:

Criterion A: Focus and method	■ select and explore an ethical dilemma embedded in an issue linked to a career-related context ■ select and apply appropriate research methods and collect and select relevant information from a variety of sources, showing an understanding of bias and validity
Criterion B: Knowledge and understanding in context	■ demonstrate knowledge and understanding of the issue ■ contextualize the ethical dilemma and analyse different perspectives on it through the use of a local/global example of the issue in which the dilemma is embedded ■ demonstrate awareness and understanding of the impact of the ethical dilemma on a local/global community and the cultural influences on, and perceptions of, the ethical dilemma
Criterion C: Critical thinking	■ demonstrate logical reasoning processes and the ability to interpret, analyse and evaluate material ■ develop the ability to synthesize information, making connections and linking ideas and evidence
Criterion D: Communication	■ present a structured and coherent project, use appropriate terminology accurately and consistently, and communicate ideas and concepts clearly
Criterion E: Engagement and reflections on planning and progress	■ reflect on and refine the research process, and react to insights gained through exploration of the ethical dilemma ■ critique decisions made throughout the research process and suggest improvements to their own working practices

■ A note on Option 2

We have discussed that it is completely your choice which option you choose for your reflective project and you might have particular talents or interests that lead you to Option 2. You will notice that this book is written in chronological order to reflect the process of the reflective project from initial ideas to final submission. The book is also led by the criteria A–E that need to go in all reflective projects and RPPFs irrespective of the option you choose. Having said this, you will undoubtedly have to have a slightly different mindset if you choose Option 2.

The key to embarking on an Option 2 reflective project is to remember throughout every stage of the process that you are working with two formats: the written report and your choice of additional format. You must make sure that these two formats complement and enhance the features of each other rather than repeat information. Once you start to feel more secure about the criteria and have mapped out your research question, area of investigation and research area (explored in Chapters 3–6) consider your additional format more closely: What elements of the criteria would it really draw out? How can the written report and the additional format complement each other?

Chapter 7 looks at establishing a positive and productive relationship with your supervisor. In early sessions with your supervisor it is essential that you look at additional advice the IB released in June 2019 for students choosing Option 2 formats. It is also an opportunity to discuss exemplar material and how previous students constructed their reflective projects. Bear in mind that when it comes to demonstrating critical thinking, you need the same approach irrespective of the mode in which you present it; you might have an idea for one of the additional formats that would allow you to show off your critical thinking skills in an imaginative and original way.

There is no set order in how you complete the two parts to the project but you must have a clear plan and structure, so Chapter 11 which explores time and process management is crucial. If you choose a format such as a film, you will need to keep in mind the time this might take. It is reassuring to know you are not assessed on your technical skills; however, that does not mean it will not be time-consuming – not only to put together but also to ensure you are as clear and consistent as possible across all the criteria. It is important to communicate with your supervisor and establish key deadlines that might help you a little more in the juggling of two formats.

> **EXPERT TIP**
>
> The most important question to have a clear answer to is: what would be the purpose in using two modalities?

> **EXPERT TIP**
>
> You might consider that one format is the perfect place to talk about multiple perspectives in far more detail or perhaps the place to explore visually the similarities and differences between local and global contexts. Equally, one of the formats might be an excellent forum to develop and debate your understanding of bias and validity of sources.

What is academic honesty?

Academic honesty is the beating heart of the whole IB framework and crucial throughout every step of the reflective project.

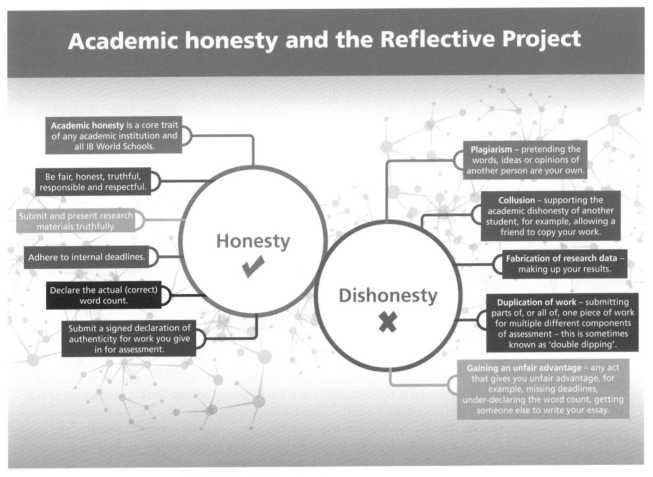

Academic honesty and the Reflective Project

Academic honesty is a core trait of any academic institution and all IB World Schools.

Be fair, honest, truthful, responsible and respectful.

Submit and present research materials truthfully.

Adhere to internal deadlines.

Declare the actual (correct) word count.

Submit a signed declaration of authenticity for work you give in for assessment.

Honesty ✔

Dishonesty ✘

Plagiarism – pretending the words, ideas or opinions of another person are your own.

Collusion – supporting the academic dishonesty of another student, for example, allowing a friend to copy your work.

Fabrication of research data – making up your results.

Duplication of work – submitting parts of, or all of, one piece of work for multiple different components of assessment – this is sometimes known as 'double dipping'.

Gaining an unfair advantage – any act that gives you unfair advantage, for example, missing deadlines, under-declaring the word count, getting someone else to write your essay.

The rules of academic honesty are crucial, clear cut and detailed. Source: Artwork from *Extended Essay: Skills for Success*, Hodder Education, 2017

ACTIVITY: ACADEMIC HONESTY

With a partner, consider every aspect of your IBCP course so far and think of how academic honesty plays a role in each one. What would be the repercussions for not being academically honest?

From what you know about the reflective project process so far, come up with five pieces of advice for keeping academically honest during the reflective project process.

Possibly stating the obvious, but the most important aspect of the reflective project, just like other assessments, is that it is entirely your work. You might be tempted to skim over this section, as just like the majority of students, you do not intend to do anything other than produce your own work. However, it is really important that you do not just understand what the concept of academic honesty is, but also what you might do to ensure your work is as authentic as possible every step of the reflective project process.

■ Keeping honest throughout the reflective project process

1 **Communicate:** Your supervisor is there to support you throughout the whole process and the more they understand your research and the way you are working, the more they can possibly help you to avoid problems. After all, they are the ones who will mark your work and you both will be asked to verify that the work is yours.

2 **Research:** Make a note of the 'who, what, why, when, where' of every article/ book/interview/website you use; this also makes the bibliography so much easier to manage. Note down information accurately at the time, as you will not remember later. Chapter 6 Research methods will help you maintain clarity in your work.

3   **Research to writing:** The analysis, evaluation and reflection of a wide range of sources must be entirely your own so make sure that all the sources you used to build your ideas are really clear to the reader; otherwise, even if unintended, this is plagiarism.

4   **Writing:** Sometimes it is easy to get carried away and use an extensive part of a source or long quote, as it all seems relevant. If you let a particular source dominate, it takes away from your own voice and therefore stops analysis from taking place. More seriously, it can be deemed as plagiarism with plagiarism software that your school and the IB use.

5   **Review and reflect:** Check your first and final draft thoroughly against your original research as once you have submitted your final draft, it cannot be changed or returned.

ACTIVITY: REFLECTION

Everyone, in any area of study, must consciously commit to academic honesty. Consider some of the areas academic honesty might play a part in the reflective project process here.

Which areas do you think you will find most challenging? Can you think of other areas of life where academic honesty might play a key role?

ACTIVITY: LEARNER PROFILE ATTRIBUTES

Now that you have been introduced to the reflective project, look at the learner profile below and consider how each characteristic might be important in the reflective project process. You can record your thoughts in a medium of your choice; be sure not to miss out a characteristic and feel free to go back over the chapter to help develop your ideas.

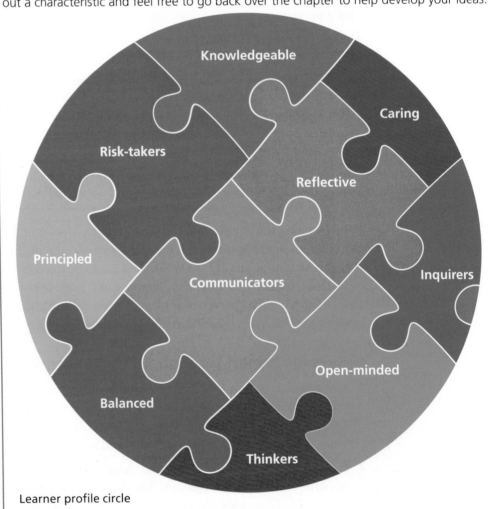

Learner profile circle

CHAPTER SUMMARY KEY POINTS

- The reflective project is a compulsory element of the IBCP core, entirely student driven. You will be assessed on the process as well as the end product.

- You have a choice of formats you can take and your school will support whichever one you want to explore. Take time to explore these choices and how you might approach them.

- You are assessed by five criteria each weighted differently, out of a total of 36 marks.

- Lastly, but most importantly, academic honesty is integral throughout the entire reflective project; take time to understand what academic malpractice can look like, the consequences involved and how to work in a way to ensure against it.

INITIAL REFLECTIONS

- What was your motivation for choosing this area?
- How did you come up with your question?
- What problems do you envisage … and what initial course of action did you follow?
- What thoughts and discussions did you have?
- Own perception/prejudices/preconceived ideas?
- What was your response to your initial discussions with your supervisor?
- How did it make you respond and feel?
- Were there other factors that influenced the situation?

INTERIM REFLECTIONS

- What have you learned from the experience so far and what is the thinking behind your next move?
- Have you had to make any modifications or change your approach?
- What setbacks have you had and how did you turn it around? ('setbacks' might be quality of source material)
- How is this experience matching with your preconceived ideas? Is the outcome so far expected or unexpected?

FINAL REFLECTIONS

- How do you respond to the ethical dilemma now you have completed the project?
- What has surprised/not surprised you most?
- What do you think might have changed the outcome?
- Would you take a different approach now, in view of the outcome?

'As the busy world spins frantically, time to reflect feels like a gift – ancient cultures have known this and made meditation part of their day. For me as an educator, reflection is when the learning happens – what did I do, how well did it go and what would I do differently next time? If you don't reflect, you repeat mistakes and don't learn. And when my reflections are confusing or unclear, then I know I've hit the learning zone!'

Carolyn, Educator and PhD candidate

'However senior you are within your chosen career, the day you believe reflection is no longer necessary is the day you should consider retiring. Reflection on all aspects of your job is essential and shows you care not only about the work itself but also about those you work with, their perception of you and ultimately therefore your own self worth.'

Emma, Solicitor

'Reflection is about having the space to consider what your skill set is and giving serious thought to what you want to do with your life. Looking back now, I wish I had been given the opportunity to experience variety at the age where I had the maturity to understand that what I naturally gravitated towards was probably what I should be concentrating on. You just can't give proper consideration to where your talents lie or what your career path might look like if you cut off your choices too early on. Specialize too soon and this valuable opportunity for reflection gets cut short.'

Lucy, Freelance writer

2 Reflection

Reflection: The RPPF and the RRS

The importance of reflection

■ Why is reflection so important?

In short, the process of reflection is such an important skill to develop that this element of the CP core was named after it. It might seem strange to start this process by discussing a word often associated with looking back on something that has finished, but a good understanding of what reflection entails at the very start of the project will get you into the mindset and working habits needed for success far beyond the parameters of the project itself.

As you know from the Introduction, this is a piece of work which asks you to analyse the multiple perspectives and evidence surrounding an ethical dilemma and come to your own conclusions. However, it is also about your understanding of the long process you went through to create your work and this is assessed separately from the rest of your project in Criterion E. As the skills you need for this project are developed over the entire IBCP course, you could say the reflective project directly and indirectly showcases how you have developed in every aspect of your course.

■ Definitions of 'reflection' and 'reflective'

When you suspect certain words are going to be used endlessly, and the words 'reflection' and 'reflective' are definitely two of them, it helps not only to revisit the definition but also to consider its synonyms. This creates a fuller view of what that word can mean and all its implications.

Out of multiple meanings, there are two that are important here. The first definition is possibly the most general and the one you are most familiar with. However, if you take a close look at the second with its synonyms of 'viewpoint', 'belief' and 'thought', you will start to notice something important; actually, the whole project is about your analysis of other people's reflections as well as your own.

DEFINITION

reflection

1　serious thought or consideration

Synonyms: thought, thinking, consideration, contemplation, study, deliberation, pondering, meditation, musing, rumination, cogitation, brooding, agonizing

2　an idea about something, especially one that is written down or expressed

Synonyms: opinion, thought, view, viewpoint, belief, feeling, idea, impression, conclusion, judgement, assessment, comment, observation, remark, statement, pronouncement, declaration

---

ACTIVITY: CHOOSING THE RIGHT WORDS

Look at the synonyms above. How do the words differ from each other? Which ones are most appropriate for discussing ethical issues and dilemmas? Which ones are familiar or help your understanding the most?

Well done – you have completed one of your first reflections; you have given thought and assessed the strengths and weaknesses of an idea before coming to your own conclusion.

■ The Reflections on planning and progress form (RPPF)

This is an assessed document separate to your main project in Criterion E and contributes up to 6 marks to your final grade. You will see an example over the page. Here you will write three reflections on your development at the beginning, middle and end of your reflective project's completion. It is important for academic honesty too, as by recording the process, it provides further evidence that your work is authentic.

The Reflections on Planning and Progress Form + meetings with your supervisor =

Criterion E: Engagement and reflection on planning and progress.

RP/RPPF

For first assessment in 2018 Candidate personal code: [   ]

Reflective project - Reflections on planning and progress

The completion of this form is a mandatory requirement of the Reflective Project from first assessment May 2018. It must be uploaded together with the completed Reflective Project for assessment under criterion E.

Candidate: This form records reflections on your planning and progress, and the nature of your discussions with your supervisor. You must undertake three formal meetings with your supervisor. These meetings will inform each of your reflections below. The first formal meeting should focus on your initial ideas and how you plan to undertake your research; the interim meeting is once a significant amount of your research has been completed, and the final meeting once you have completed and handed in your reflective project.

After each formal meeting you must record your reflections on this form and your supervisor must sign and date each reflection. This form acts as a record in supporting the authenticity of your work. Please refer to assessment criterion E in the reflective project guide when completing this form.

The three reflections combined must amount to no more than 1,000 words.

Supervisor: You must have at least three meetings with each candidate, one early on in the process, an interim meeting and then the final meeting. Other meetings are permitted but do not need to be recorded on this sheet. After each formal meeting candidates must record their reflections and as the supervisor you must sign and date this form.

First reflection
Candidate reflections:

RP/RPPF
Interim reflection
Candidate reflections:

Date: [   ]   Supervisor initials: [   ]

Final reflection

Candidate reflections:

Date: [   ]   Supervisor initials: [   ]

RP/RPPF

Supervisor comments:

Source: International Baccalaureate Organization, 2019

Informed by your meetings with your supervisor, here you will document:

■ initial ideas

■ any concerns

■ outcome of discussions with your supervisor

■ interim thoughts about the reflective project's planning, progress and content

■ any changes that need to be made to complete the project

■ finishing the project and your final conclusions.

The RPPF is NOT: Somewhere to repeat the content of the reflective project itself.

The RRPF IS: An opportunity to reflect on difficulties encountered, how they were overcome and what was learned in the process.

■ A 'researcher's reflection space' (RRS)

You need the RRS to complete the RPPF successfully as it is a record of your progress. This is not assessed but is a central process to the reflective project as it is a place where you can ponder your topic and the way it is developing. The RRS is a long journey with potential for wrong turns and dead ends, but you will get to your destination.

How can I reflect?

The nature of the IBCP means that you will have many commitments and will need to be able to pick up regularly where you left off with the reflective project process in the time you have set aside; a consistent RRS will make this far quicker and you will be more motivated to work on it.

Putting time aside for your RRS can help make reflecting a natural thought process for you. It is here that you can take a step back from your research and make personal reflections on the progress, discoveries, frustrations, not to mention strengths and weaknesses of ideas you encounter – you will notice just how the learner profile attributes help in your development. The RRS will not only help you chart your research and write your RPPF but it will also make sessions with your supervisor purposeful. The more you ask questions and record your thoughts as you go along, the more your project will be led by you and your personal voice will come through in your critical analysis.

■ What will your researcher's reflection space (RRS) look like?

First, your RRS will be full of your questions; you will have initial questions but the more you find out about your topic, the more questions you will have. Second, your RRS will be a space to record information and your thoughts; just like you will discover a topic you find interesting, you need to find a way of recording your research and reflections that interests you just as much. The IB reflective project student guide recommends a journal or a blog and a host of different methods you could use within it.

> **EXPERT TIP**
>
> At the end of a research and reflection session, write a short summary of your findings and/or further questions that you might now have. This will make it easy for you to know where to start next time and be far more efficient.

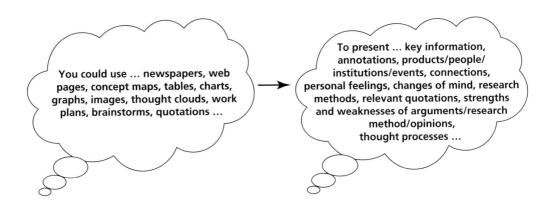

You could use … newspapers, web pages, concept maps, tables, charts, graphs, images, thought clouds, work plans, brainstorms, quotations …

To present … key information, annotations, products/people/institutions/events, connections, personal feelings, changes of mind, research methods, relevant quotations, strengths and weaknesses of arguments/research method/opinions, thought processes …

EXAMPLE TASK: USING THE RRS FOR INITIAL PLANNING

Questions in your RRS – What topics have I found most interesting in my career-related subject (CRS)? What areas do I find interesting that I have not studied? What has been the outcome of discussions and activities in PPS? What do I know already about this? Do I understand the ethical issues behind this topic? Can I see where there might be an ethical dilemma? Could this area be too broad or too narrow to research?

RRS tools you might use – A mind map of questions, interesting photos annotated with questions or initial thoughts, two newspaper articles that seem to agree or disagree with each other and your bullet points of connections and your thoughts.

ACTIVITY: DEFINING YOUR RESEARCH AND REFLECTIONS SPACE (RRS)

Which method/s work best for you? Which are most important? Try to picture how you would like to see your research build and what form it might take. How will you use visual or written methods? How will you signpost key developments? Are there any that are not here?

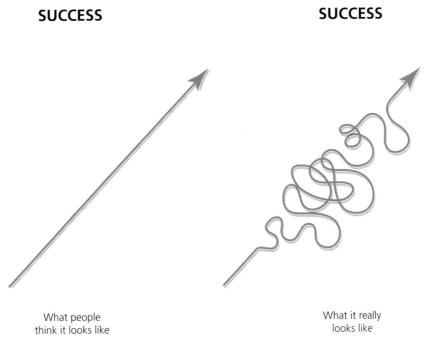

SUCCESS

SUCCESS

What people think it looks like

What it really looks like

Which one represents a successful reflective project?

ACTIVITY: CREATE A DATABASE OF QUESTIONS

Create a database of questions that will help you reflect along the way in your RRS. There are some to get you started in the infographic on pages 12–13 but try doing this exercise first.

Question starters: what, when, why, how, where, if, should, could …

Question topics: initial ideas, predictions, sources, surprises, disappointments, successes, setbacks, new directions, adaptations, strengths, weaknesses, personal obstacles and successes.

EXAMPLE TASK: WHAT DO YOUR QUESTIONS REVEAL?

Now look at your questions – do they take into account the learner profile attributes?

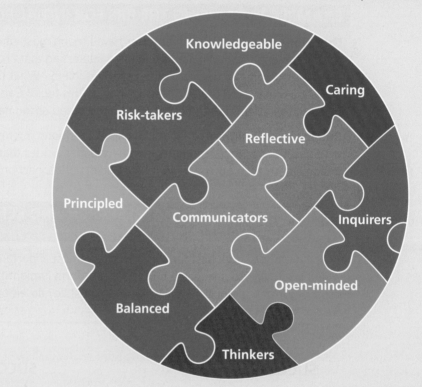

ACTIVITY: BECOME AN INTERVIEWER

A good way of testing your reflective questions is to use them to interview people both from your career-related context and outside it. Interview an adult about their career and ask them the questions you have created as well as ones from the following topics: education and career path; successes and setbacks; the learner profile's significance; and importance of lifelong learning.

ACTIVITY: INTERVIEW REFLECTION

Record your findings from the interview by creating a visual reminder in your RRS. You might present your findings about what you learned from your interviewee about each of the topics and reflect on which questions brought about the best answers. Take a step back and consider more generally what you learned from interviewing a professional outside of your school context. What surprised you? What interested you? Did you empathize with any of their observations?

Relevant assessment criteria

It is worth looking at Criterion E and the standards for achieving the highest grade for reflection (5–6 marks). Look at the words in bold in particular; reflective skills of this level can be developed through the recommended activities on page 20.

- There is evidence that student reflection is **evaluative**.

- Reflections given on decision-making and planning include reference to **the student's capacity to consider actions and ideas in response to setbacks** experienced in the research process.

- These reflections communicate a **high degree of intellectual and personal engagement with the subject and process of research, demonstrating authenticity, intellectual initiative and/or creativity in the student voice.**

CHAPTER SUMMARY KEY POINTS

- Being reflective is a key attribute of the IB learner profile.

- Reflection is a compulsory part of the reflective project and is formally assessed.

- While not assessed, it is crucial to keep a consistent Researcher's Reflection Space (RRS).

- All IBCP students are required to complete a Reflections on Planning and Progress Form (RPPF) which is assessed with your reflective project.

- The RPPF is worth 6 marks.

- A blank or missing RPPF will achieve zero marks in Criterion E.

- There are three mandatory reflection sessions with your supervisor:
  - Initial reflection session, with a focus on establishing the issue, dilemma and question and research method.
  - Interim reflection, with a focus on challenges and changes you have made as well as reflection on your first draft.
  - Final reflection, with a focus on your final draft and an overview of how your perceptions have been challenged over the whole process.

Defining the investigation

5.
Focused ethical dilemma
Now proceed to the checklist to see if you can make it the focus of your whole reflective project.

4. **Ethical dilemmas**
Using your understanding of an ethical dilemma, pick five of the most interesting issues you have discovered and consider which dilemmas arise from them. Or there might be one issue with a variety of dilemmas arising from it. Which are the most interesting dilemmas? Pick the one you most want to explore more at this stage.

3. **Ethical issues in areas of interest**
Using your understanding of an ethical issue, take each area of interest and create a mind map of issues that arise from it.

2. **Areas of interest**
Come up with five areas of general interest connected with your CRS. Find images to accompany them.

1. **Career-related subject**
What is your career-related subject?
What subtopics within your CRS are there?

START HERE

Checklist

To be ready to start your reflective project, you need to be able to answer yes to each question.

1. Are you clear on the difference between an ethical issue and dilemma? ☐

2. Can you explain the issue you are exploring and the specific dilemma arising from it? ☐

3. Is the solution to the ethical dilemma not straightforward or obvious? ☐

4. Can you identify multiple (3+) perspectives or stakeholders you could explore in connection with the dilemma? ☐

5. Do you have a reflective project focused on an ethical dilemma and not the issue? ☐

LEARNER PROFILE ATTRIBUTES		
Communicator	Reflective	Open-minded
Inquirer	Thinker	

Introduction

■ Defining a clear goal and student ownership; choosing an ethical issue that interests you

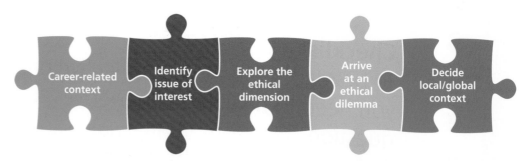

Taking ownership of your reflective project starts with choosing an ethical issue that interests you. It may sound extreme but you have a duty to get this right; take time and be patient, as you will not regret the time spent on this. However, there are further responsibilities to take on board and understanding the implications of these early on for your specific learner profile will lead you to have complete ownership of this project.

ACTIVITY: TAKING RESPONSIBILITY

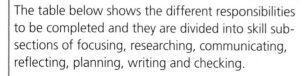

The table below shows the different responsibilities to be completed and they are divided into skill sub-sections of focusing, researching, communicating, reflecting, planning, writing and checking.

Which ones might you find easiest or most difficult to complete? Could any responsibilities belong in more than one area? What characteristics of the learner profile will you have to call upon at specific stages?

Focusing	• Choose an issue arising from your career-related studies that presents an ethical dilemma.
Researching	• Record sources as you carry out the research. • Keep consistently a 'researcher's reflection space' to reflect upon your progress and create the structure of your scheduled meetings with the supervisor.
Communicating	• Discuss the ethical dilemma with your supervisor. • Meet both internal and external assessment deadlines set by your school and the IB. • Inform your supervisor of details of any external assistance received.
Reflecting	• Complete the RPPF as the work progresses, and after each of the scheduled meetings with your supervisor. NOT at the end.
Planning	• Plan ahead. • Create a schedule for researching and producing the reflective project but also anticipate delays and unforeseen problems. • Plan how you will find varied material for your research. • Develop an appropriately focused research question. • Have a clear structure before beginning to write.

Writing	• State explicitly how your questions link to your career-related study at the start of your reflective project.
	• Acknowledge all sources of information and ideas in references, citations and bibliography.
Checking	• Address the assessment criteria fully.
	• Carefully check and proofread the final version of the reflective project. Ensure that all basic requirements are met.

See Chapter 11 for more detail on time management and planning.

Why is an ethical education so important?

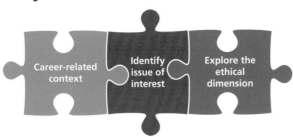

The reflective project is a vehicle for exploring ethical dilemmas in real-life situations. Why is this important? Before even starting to decide on the focus of your reflective project, it is important to lay the foundations of why an ethical education is wholly relevant to you. After all, the IBCP core is all about helping you forge your own identities and principles to take forward into your future. The importance of an ethical education is felt by many different professions. For example, consider the following viewpoint from the world of science.

'Today, ethics has an important place in all areas of life. Education is also a fundamental process of human life. Therefore, in education ethics has a very important and effective role. In order to be a good human, ethics should be placed as a course in [the] educational system.'

Source: www.sciencedirect.com/science/article/pii/S1877042815009945

ACTIVITY: THE ROLE OF AN ETHICAL EDUCATION

You will find here different perspectives from real professionals about the significance of ethics in the workplace. All of them demonstrate that an ethical education prepares you for the decisions you may have to make or be part of beyond the classroom whether in a personal or professional setting.

'Day-to-day life requires constant decision-making which can have short- and long-term consequences for individual, group and wider societal outcomes.' **Claire, Social Worker**

'If I don't ask the right questions, my whole business is compromised.' *Jonny, CEO of Digital Communications Agency*

'It's not about what's right and wrong but the multidimensional nature of the workplace that's important and discovering where you stand.' *Michelle, Solicitor*

'An ethical education is a large part of that which shapes the kind of adult you will become. A good grounding in ethics can be passed on in the form of informed advice. Thereby helping, with good conscience, the next generation understand their struggles from an experienced point of view.' **Jonathan, Creative Director**

Which ones do you think apply most to your chosen career-related study?

Ethical principles

Key into a search engine the words 'Ethical Principles' and you will see many examples of fundamental principles that form the basis of ethical study, as well as information on the ethical principles that underpin many professions by providing the framework within which dilemmas can be analysed. The number of principles might vary slightly but very often contain **respecting autonomy, doing no harm, benefiting others, being just** and **being faithful**. The following extract gives an idea about how different professions apply certain ethical principles within their given context as well as more detail on these ethical principles.

Ethical principles provide a generalized framework within which particular ethical dilemmas may be analysed in our daily lives. These principles may be applied to our interpersonal relationships as well as to our professional lives. However, as members of a profession, we will encounter more specific codes of ethics that are designed to govern our professional behaviour and to offer some guidance for the resolution of commonly faced ethical issues that occur in the practice of our chosen professions. What follows are definitions of five ethical principles that have been applied within a number of professions.

- **Respecting autonomy:** the individual has the right to act as a free agent. That is, human beings are free to decide how they live their lives as long as their decisions do not negatively impact the lives of others. Human beings also have the right to exercise freedom of thought or choice.
- **Doing no harm (Nonmaleficence):** Our interactions with people (within the helping professions or otherwise) should not harm others. We should not engage in any activities that run the risk of harming others.
- **Benefiting others (Beneficence):** Our actions should actively promote the health and well-being of others.
- **Being just (Justice):** In the broadest sense of the word, this means being fair. This is especially the case when the rights of one individual or group are balanced against another. Being just, however, assumes three standards. They are impartiality, equality, and reciprocity (based on the golden rule: treat others as you wish to be treated).
- **Being faithful (Fidelity):** Being faithful involves loyalty, truthfulness, promise keeping, and respect. This principle is related to the treatment of autonomous people. Failure to remain faithful in dealing with others denies individuals the full opportunity to exercise free choice in a relationship, therefore limiting their autonomy.

Source: *Principles of Biomedical ethics*, TL Beauchamp and JF Childress, 1979, Oxford University Press.

EXPERT TIP

From the start, practise exploring a range of alternative words for 'ethical' and 'moral' to add variety to your ideas and discussions.

Throughout your PPS lessons you will be guided through ethical principles and challenged increasingly by the ethical dimensions to different areas of your course, your own life and the wider world. Being open-minded to new ideas will allow you to find out where you stand on issues and be empathetic to the views of others.

What are ethics and morals?

Let's go back to the start and look at a number of definitions in the field of ethics that are particularly relevant to the reflective project. There is a danger in your studies that you will use words such as 'ethics' and 'ethical' so much that you lose sight of what they actually mean, so it is a good idea to consider synonyms to give you a wider vocabulary as well as understanding.

What does ethics really mean?

DEFINITIONS

Ethics:

1 the standards of right and wrong

2 a set of moral principles that govern a person's behaviour or the conducting of an activity

Synonyms: moral code, morality, moral stand, moral principles, moral values, rights and wrongs, ideals, creed, standards, virtues

Ethical:

1 relating to moral principles or the branch of knowledge dealing with these

Synonyms: moral, social, behavioural, having to do with right and wrong

2 morally good or correct

Synonyms: right-minded, right-thinking, principled, irreproachable, unimpeachable, blameless, guiltless, righteous, upright, upstanding, good, lawful, honest, trustworthy, admirable, praiseworthy

Morals:

1 standards of behaviour; principles of right and wrong

Synonyms: moral code, code of ethics, moral standards, moral values, principles, principles of right and wrong, rules of conduct, standards/principles of behaviour, standards, morality, sense of morality, scruples, ideals

■ Why is the distinction between ethics and morals important?

'Ethics and morals relate to "right" and "wrong". While they are sometimes used interchangeably, they are different: ethics refer to rules provided by an external source e.g. sources of conduct in workplaces or principles in religions. Morals refer to an individual's own principles regarding right and wrong.'

Source: www.diffen.com/difference/Ethics_vs_Morals

Can you see this distinction? In terms of the reflective project, you will be exploring a range of individuals' moral perspectives in relation to how they are challenged by a particular ethical context.

■ What is an ethical dimension, issue and dilemma?

Further to understanding the difference between ethics and morals is the further distinction between ethical dimensions, issues and dilemmas.

DEFINITIONS

Ethical dimension:

1   the range of moral aspects related to a topic

Ethical issue:

1   an important topic or problem for debate or discussion

Synonyms: matter, subject, topic, question, concern, situation, circumstance

Ethical dilemma:

1   a situation in which a difficult choice has to be made between two or more alternatives, especially ones that are equally undesirable; there may be no right or wrong answer

Synonyms: quandary, predicament, difficulty, problem, puzzle, conundrum

Controversial:

1   giving rise or likely to give rise to controversy or public disagreement

Synonyms: contentious, disputed, contended, debatable, arguable, open to discussion/question, emotive, sensitive, delicate, difficult, awkward, problematic

ACTIVITY: DIMENSIONS, ISSUES AND DILEMMAS

Investigate different ethical dimensions and start to discuss examples of the differences between an issue and a dilemma. Explore the ethical and moral issues discussed in the following online journal:

New Scientist: **www.newscientist.com/round-up/ethics-issue**

You could consider the definitions and synonyms above, as well as identify your own perspectives on the examples given. Remember, for it to be an ethical dilemma, there must be a clash of principles so look for the clash.

ACTIVITY: CREATE AN ETHICAL FORUM

Organize a forum to discuss current topics and debates within your career-related subject, inviting your teachers, supervisors and any relevant stakeholders (other students, parents, governors, community members) you think would contribute well to the discussion. You might start by discussing the difference between an issue and a dilemma, as many people find this distinction difficult no matter who they are.

■ Recognizing key communities and contexts

What will make your reflective project even more interesting for you and make it stand out is if you choose dynamic local and global examples that relate to your ethical dilemma. It is also an important step in enabling you to analyse an ethical dilemma from multiple perspectives and its real-world impact.

Your ethical dilemma will be focused on a particular community or group of people. Your local/global example will link to it in specific ways relevant to your area of study, such as by ethnicity, geography or religion. You might have already chosen an area to explore and have direct experience that provides a local example; it might be an example of a community on the other side of the world experiencing something in a similar or different way to something you have come across in your initial reading. Whatever the examples, make them original, as these will reinforce your ideas and help you consider your ideas from new angles. Furthermore, examples that are focused and really appropriate to your study will develop your critical understanding far more.

EXPERT TIP

From the very start, ask yourself: Why does this topic matter to me, people around me, and the wider world?

Finding your own issue and dilemma

■ Identify prior knowledge

It has already been stressed that you must choose an area that interests you for your reflective project. However, you do not necessarily need to start from scratch but consider what you already know and build upon it. How do you go about this?

- You already have a sizeable amount of subject-specific knowledge retained from your career-related subject (CRS) and this learning connects with other areas of knowledge and influences to form your unique perception of it. The learning we retain the most is often what we find most interesting.

- You might connect your CRS directly with other subjects you already have an interest in. For example, your CRS might be Business or Art and Design, or you might take Business Studies or Art for your DP subject. How might these worlds connect?

- Equally, you might have interests outside of your studies which might connect with your CRS brilliantly.

■ Approaches to defining your reflective project

The following activities are designed to help you define the area of study for your reflective project by encouraging you to uncover your own voice and viewpoints.

Lead your project with a confident voice

ACTIVITY 1: FINDING YOUR VOICE

Explore the issue on this NGO website: **www.amnesty.org/en/what-we-do/**

What dilemmas are depicted? Look for a clash of ethical principles. Think about the different perspectives there might be. What do you think?

ACTIVITY 2: PLACE YOURSELF IN THE ETHICAL DIMENSION

What is happening in the photo? What assumptions can you make? Why do you think that? Where do your sympathies lie?

Research the origin of the photo using the internet; you might make use of the suggested key words at the end of activity 3 on page 31 or your own observations. Now place yourself in the shoes of two or three people in the picture. Try and see matters from their perspective, even if you do not agree.

ACTIVITY 3: TURNING INTERESTS TO ISSUES AND DILEMMAS

This activity has three stages. Either working by yourself, or in a small group with people from other career-related subjects to your own, cover a space of wall with a sizeable amount of large paper. In the following exercise, try to include as many of your own interests and thoughts as possible no matter how unconnected you think they might be to your CRS – this is about creating; you will select and refine later. If you are working with others, take turns to support each other and talk through each of your ideas.

Stage 1: Circles of Interests

1   Draw three circles within each other – small, medium and large.

2   Beginning in the centre circle, start mind mapping the different areas of your CRS you have studied so far and any sub-topics that come to mind.

3   In the next circle, put in the areas you find particularly interesting – you do not need to know why yet – and be sure to use a different colour for each person.

4   In the outer circle, put in areas connected with your CRS that you may not have studied yet or will not study but you are interested in.

Circle the areas that interest you the most. These might be different global or local contexts that interest you or real-life situations. Chat to your group about the mind map you have produced. Please note if you do work with others that they are from different career-related contexts as it can be difficult to remain academically honest otherwise.

Remember to take a photo for your RRS, which you can annotate with any further thoughts.

Stage 2: From Circles of Interest to identifying ethical issues

Look for the controversy

Sometimes, it just takes one word to get you to an important matter associated with your career-related subject. To uncover ethical issues you might want to explore more – see how the following words might connect with your ideas from the last exercise.

Responsibility	**Duty**	**Protection**	Conflict	**Control**	Freedom
Equality	Authority	**Law**	**Money**	**Funding**	**Education**
Government	**Charity**	**Censorship**	Age	Love	**Prejudice**
Hate					

Stage 3: Uncovering the dilemmas

Expand on the ideas you like the most by considering:

1 What you know already.

2 What questions you have (you might have ALL questions).

3 Are there two or more stakeholders and who might they be?

4 What might be the different perspectives of these stakeholders?

5 What is your initial perspective?

6 What is a stakeholder?

Differentiating a dilemma from an issue can be difficult. However, if you can find at least two perspectives that show different moral points of view connected with the topic you have uncovered, you are on your way.

Look at the reflection point on page 33 to check your understanding further.

The following example reflects a common ethical issue in society nowadays. The clash of the right of the employer vs the right of the individual. Can you see any other clashes at play?

Dilemma: Should employers be allowed to monitor employees' activity on their computers and company-provided devices?

Look for the clash of ethical principles in a dilemma

■ Relevant assessment criteria development

Here are the criteria for achieving the highest band of Criterion B: Knowledge and Understanding. Think about how you have been using these during this chapter then try the activity below.

- The central ethical dilemma is analysed from different perspectives, which are evaluated in a balanced way. Overall, the work demonstrates a considered and developed knowledge and understanding of the ethical dilemma with a clear sense of scope and context(s).

- The use of a local or global example to contextualize the ethical dilemma is effective and well integrated.

- The impact of the ethical dilemma on community members is analysed and forms an integral part of the inquiry.

- Analysis of how cultural perspectives can influence the ethical dilemma is developed and integrated into the ideas presented.

REFLECTION POINT

A five-minute analysis of an ethical dilemma as a pair or a group.

This is a quick blast activity to see how quickly you can identify the key features of a dilemma. Look at the following dilemma and answer the questions underneath. You have five minutes before sharing your ideas.

What is the ethical dilemma? *Should we colonize other planets?*

What is the clash? *Realize human potential vs Minimize suffering of other life forms*

What is the clash of ethical principles? *Benefiting others vs Doing no harm*
- What are the **initial questions**?
- What **information** do you need?
- Who are the key **stakeholders** and what might they think?
- What are the **implications and practical consequences** of this issue?

CHAPTER SUMMARY KEY POINTS

- It is crucial you choose an ethical issue that interests you and will keep you interested over a long period of time.

- Before embarking on your project, identify what you know already.

- Work hard on establishing the difference between an ethical issue and an ethical dilemma as the success of your reflective project will rely on this understanding.

- Your reflective project will take on its own identity when you recognize key communities and contexts; take time to look into the diversity of your ethical dilemma.

The Importance of

'A moral being is one who is capable of comparing his past and future actions or motives, and of approving or disapproving of them.'

Charles Darwin

'We children of public school age can do much to aid in the promotion of peace. We must try to train ourselves and those about us to live together with one another as good neighbors for this idea is embodied in the great new Charter of the United Nations. It is the only way to secure the world against future wars and maintain an everlasting peace.'

Ruth Bader Ginsburg

'The only way I can pay back for what fate and society have handed me is to try, in minor totally useless ways, to make an angry sound against injustice.'

Martha Gellhorn

'Whatever is my right as a man is also the right of another; and it becomes my duty to guarantee as well as to possess.'

Thomas Paine

'There is nothing radical about moral clarity.'

Alexandria Ocasio-Cortez

Ethics in society

'Men, in general, seem to employ their reason to justify prejudices ... rather than to root them out.'

Mary Wollstonecraft

'A man's ethical behaviour should be based effectually on sympathy, education, and social ties and needs; no religious basis is necessary. Man would indeed be in a poor way if he had to be restrained by fear of punishment and hope of reward after death.'

Albert Einstein

'I am a thinker, and I do muse over things a lot and am constantly assessing whether I am doing enough or what I should be doing more of to make sure I am not letting anyone down.'

Jacinda Ardern

'What we think, or what we know, or what we believe is, in the end, of little consequence. The only consequence is what we do.'

John Ruskin

'If we aren't willing to pay a price for our values, then we should ask ourselves whether we truly believe in them at all.'

Barack Obama

4 Investigating ethical dimensions

Why do we explore ethical theories?

As human beings, we know we feel strongly about issues such as human rights, euthanasia, war and globalization, or at least hold opinions, but we don't reflect about how we came to that stance. And when we don't know *why* we think something, it becomes hard to justify or expand on our ideas.

Discussion and debate can come to a grinding halt when someone falls back on a defensive stance of 'well, it's my opinion'. As an IBCP student, thinking deeply about why you think the way you do is not necessarily a comfortable process. However, when you ask questions and consider even just a few philosophical theories in their application to ethical dilemmas, you will not only come to a new understanding of what you think and why you think it, you might find new ideas. You will find your voice.

Work out where you stand ethically

So, understanding ethical issues is not about there being a single, right answer. It is about recognizing that when a set of principles is applied in a specific situation, it not only gives choice to those involved but can clarify issues to the extent that an individual can decide what they think is right.

The three branches of ethics

Exploring alternative systems of thoughts is central to being an open-minded critical thinker. The purpose of this section is not to go into vast detail on a mass of ethical theories; it is specifically to encourage the process of applying knowledge and understanding and critical thinking by taking a few influential examples as a starting point and seeing what happens if you them apply to real-world ethical quandaries.

If you explore how a particular theoretical stance could promote a certain course of action and perspective, it can help you understand why different stakeholders think and act they way they do in relation to the issue and dilemma at the heart of your reflective project. Weighing up the strengths and weaknesses of these perspectives will add depth to your argument and also help you find possible solutions. It is an interesting process as it might uncover thoughts and opinions you might not have known that you had. Looking through the lens of different perspectives in your reflective project will give you a framework to develop your ideas into original and complex reasoning.

There are three branches of ethics to understand:

- **Meta-ethics** studies the meanings of ethical terms, the nature of ethical judgments, and types of ethical arguments. It is not concerned with the rightness and wrongness of specific acts; it asks about the nature of goodness and badness, what it is to be morally right or wrong.

- **Normative ethics** seeks to provide a general theory and framework for ethics on how we ought to live rather than tell us specific things that have moral properties. For any act there are three morally interesting factors: the agent (the person performing the act), the act itself, and the consequences. Virtue, deontological and consequentialist ethics emphasize each of these elements in turn.

- **Applied ethics** is the most practical of the three branches and essentially seeks to apply normative ethics to specific issues and situations.

ACTIVITY: ETHICAL KNOWLEDGE AND UNDERSTANDING

How are the three branches of ethics that are listed below reflected in the top band of Criterion B: Knowledge and Understanding?

- The central ethical dilemma is analysed from different perspectives, which are evaluated in a balanced way. Overall, the work demonstrates a considered and developed knowledge and understanding of the ethical dilemma with a clear sense of scope and context(s).

- The use of a local or global example to contextualize the ethical dilemma is effective and well integrated.

- The impact of the ethical dilemma on community members is analysed and forms an integral part of the inquiry.

REFLECTION POINT

Across your IBCP course so far, reflect on times when you have discussed the three branches of ethics – knowingly or unknowingly!

EXAMPLE TASK: CASE STUDY AND ACTIVITY

Meta-ethics activity: Living in Truth and Havel's Greengrocer – Research and Discussion

Vaclav Havel (1936–2011) was a famous philosopher, poet and playwright imprisoned for his beliefs during the Czechoslovakian communist era, but after its fall, he became President of Czechoslovakia and then of the Czech Republic. He wrote throughout his life on the nature of human freedom and his analogy of a Prague greengrocer in his political essay 'The power of the powerless' in his book *Living in Truth* has become famous and well worth researching as an individual, group or a class. You could read the essay itself or find shorter secondary analysis for an overview of the essay. There are obituaries for Vaclav Havel that consider his work, as well as how he lived his life. There is also an abridged presentation of the essay in this video: **https://youtu.be/oSMwrJ-KMxU**

Exploring the ethical dimension

The following theories come under the heading of 'normative ethics'. Through an emphasis on the person, the action or the consequence, they will help you explore the ethical dimensions of your focus. Remember that ethical theories are not perfect and come with strengths and weaknesses; some of these are also explored but you may well come up with more.

The person

■ The example of Aristotle's Virtue Ethics and The Golden Mean

Aristotle (384–322 BC) was a scholar in many disciplines and his moral philosophy is based around assessing the broad characters of human beings rather than assessing singular acts in isolation, which makes it different to Utilitarianism and Kantian Ethics.

Aristotle and The Golden Mean

- Aristotle uses the Greek term *eudaimonia* to capture the state that we experience if we fully achieve a good life. Eudaimonia is to be understood as 'flourishing' rather than just happiness.

- You achieve eudaimonia through desirable personality traits and character disposition called 'virtues' and act in accordance with reason.

- The focus on character makes this an 'agent-centred' moral theory rather than act-centred moral theory.

- Morality has more to do with the question 'How should I be?' rather than 'What should I do?' Take care of the first question and the second question is easily answered.

- Virtues are those particular dispositions that when are appropriately related to the situation, encourage actions that are in accordance with reason. When viewed holistically, they define our characters and who we are.

- A virtue must not be mistaken for a feeling. Virtue is a measured psychological response, neither excessive or deficient, to a feeling – this is acting on the basis of the Golden Mean.

Examples of the Golden Mean			
Feeling/Emotion	**Vice of deficiency**	**Virtuous disposition (Golden Mean)**	**Vice of excess**
Anger	Lack of spirit	Patience	Irascibility
Shame	Shyness	Modesty	Shamefulness
Fear	Cowardice	Courage	Rashness
Indignation	Spitefulness	Righteousness	Envy

Source: Adapted from: https://books.openedition.org/obp/4421?lang=en#tocfrom1n1 with reference to Aristotle, The Nicomachean Ethics, http://sacred-texts.com/cla/ari/nico/index.htm

Strengths: This refreshingly places humans, relationships and emotions of the utmost importance, unlike many theories. Ethical decisions can be based upon an individual's well-being and not just what the law might dictate as right. It is designed to equip the human at the centre of the moral dilemma with the tools to deal with it.

Criticisms: Its focus on the individual and specific traits means that it does not try to resolve big moral dilemmas or take into account the big picture. Society is complex and large; decisions need to be made taking into account the consequences of actions on the masses. The Golden Mean cannot be applied universally to all situations. Equally, it does not respect cultural distinctions; what is seen as virtuous in one country might not be seen as virtuous in another.

Source: Adapted from www.bloodyalevels.com/strengths-and-weaknesses-of-virtue-ethics/

Further reading: Here is an accessible and engaging discussion of Aristotelian Virtue Ethics:

Aristotle & Virtue Theory: Crash Course Philosophy #38 https://youtu.be/PrvtOWEXDIQ

ACTIVITY: EXPLORING VIRTUE ETHICS

Explore the examples of The Golden Mean. Do you agree with the vices of efficiency and excess? Can you think of examples you might add to the table? How might this model have a role in debating ethical issues today?

The act

■ Deontological ethics

Deontological theories of what makes an action right or wrong are concerned with actions in themselves, and not consequences: actions have an intrinsic moral value built-in to them and are right or wrong in themselves. Immanuel Kant was a very famous proponent of deontological ethics; he was born in 1724 in Prussia, never marrying and his desire for order and structure is echoed in his moral theory as well as, it seems, in his everyday life:

Purity of Intention

■ The example of Kantian Ethics

'The life of Immanuel Kant is hard to describe; he has indeed neither life nor history in the proper sense of the words. He lived an abstract, mechanical, old-bachelor existence, in a quiet remote street in Konigsberg. I do not believe that the great cathedral clock in that city accomplished a day's work in a less passionate and more regular way than its countryman, Immanuel Kant. Rising from bed, coffee-drinking, writing, lecturing, eating, walking, everything had its fixed time…'

Heinrich Heine, neighbour

- Kant believed that the only thing that was 'pure' was our **reason** (rationality) and consequences of actions were too unpredictable to measure. Equally, our feelings could be corrupted; we might act out of love in both giving to charity and a crime of passion with very different consequences.

- The only thing that makes any action good is the **motive** of the person doing it. Kant famously said that: 'Good Will shines forth like a precious jewel. It is impossible to conceive anything at all in the world, or even out of it, which can be taken as good without qualification, except a good will.'

Immanuel Kant

- Kant believed that we should always act of **duty** alone based upon the rightness or wrongness of the action. For example, to tell the truth because it is in our interest to do it isn't a moral action; however, telling the truth should be done because it is right in itself.

- Kant believed that there is an objective **moral law** and that we know this through reason. It is something that we discover, that exists independently of us, through reasoning. Morality is absolute: moral rules exist and they are binding and unchanging.

- Kant created what he called **the categorical imperative**, which is a command that is done for its own sake. Kant contrasted this with what he called hypothetical imperatives, which start with 'If...', such as, 'If I give to charity, I will be happy' and had nothing to do with morality. The only moral imperatives were categorical and, deemed right or wrong, they needed to pass the '**universal law**' made up of **three Maxims**.

  □ Maxim One: Do not act on any principle that cannot be universalized: in other words, imagine that everyone was doing what you wanted to do. If an action is right for me, it is right for everyone.

  □ Maxim Two: Treat humans as ends in themselves, not merely means. This means that we should never 'use and abuse' other people, for example to exploit or enslave them. All human beings deserve the same (good).

  □ Maxim Three: Live as if you are living in a kingdom of ends. This means that when you universalize, do so by considering other people as ends not means. It simply ties the other two maxims together.

Some possible strengths: Duty-based ethical systems emphasize the value of every human being and provide a basis of human rights considering the rights of the individual, even if at odds with the larger group. Kantian ethics dictate that some things can never be done irrespective of the consequences, which reflects the way some humans think. It is a system that takes into account the intentions and motives behind an action, which also mirrors the way people might think. It provides certainty and clear moral rules.

Some possible criticisms: Duty-based ethics set absolute rules so anything that does not seem to fit just makes a list of exceptions to the rule. The lack of interest in results or consequences means that acts could possibly be allowed that reduce the happiness of the world and most people would not see this as a viable definition of ethics.

For further explanation and examples of applying Kantian ethics access the Crash Course Philosophy lectures at: **https://www.youtube.com/watch?v=8bIys6JoEDw**

ACTIVITY: EXPLORING DEONTOLOGICAL ETHICS

What might be the strengths and weaknesses of an ethical theory that has absolute rules?

The consequence

■ Utilitarianism

Actions have consequences

Jeremy Bentham

■ The example of utilitarianism

'An action is right if it brings about more pleasure than pain and wrong if it brings more pain than pleasure.'

Jeremy Bentham

This theory is first associated with a philosopher called Jeremy Bentham and then later John Stuart Mill. Bentham argued that we can calculate how useful an action is by how much happiness it gives people. Utilitarianism is a teleological system, which means that we should choose things on the basis of the end result. The key question to ask is: what brings about the greatest good for the greatest number of people?

■ Utilitarianism is about trying to achieve happiness, so it is called a **Hedonist** system.

■ Bentham provided seven principles in **The Hedonic Calculus**, which could be used as a guide to assess how much happiness an action might produce.

1	**Intensity** of pleasure	How deep?
2	**Duration** of pleasure	How long?
3	**Certainty** of the pleasure	How likely or unlikely
4	**Remoteness** of the pleasure	How soon will it occur?
5	**Chance of succession** of the pleasure	Is it likely to be followed by similar sensations?
6	The **purity** of the pleasure	How pure will it be (is it mixed with unpleasant things)?
7	The **extent** of the pleasure	How many people will share in it?

■ John Stuart Mill adapted Bentham's approach as while he agreed that we should seek out happiness, he saw that there are **different types of happiness** in the world. He stated, 'Some kinds of pleasures are more desirable and more valuable than others, it would be absurd that while in estimating all other things, quality is not also considered as well as quantity.'

- Human pleasures are the type of pleasures that only humans can enjoy. These include things like art, music and problem solving which are **'higher' pleasures** and worth more than animal pleasure (which include things like eating). He famously said, 'It is better to be a human dissatisfied than a pig satisfied; better to be Socrates dissatisfied than a fool satisfied.'

- Mill said that since people see their own happiness as a 'good' thing, then it is equally 'good' to aim for general happiness in society. This is the principle of **universalizability**. People want to be happy so people should try and do things that make them happy and, therefore, people should try and do things that make everyone happy.

- Mill also thought that it would be necessary to have some rules for society. He said that the rules should be things, which, if followed universally, would be most likely to bring about the greatest happiness.

Some possible strengths: It might seem right that prioritizing happiness and avoiding harm is at the heart of an ethical theory. It therefore makes logical sense that the right course of action is the one that causes most happiness and least harm. It is a universal system that is not reliant on any religious beliefs so could easily cross cultural boundaries and seems to be at the heart of modern democracies. By measuring the positive and negative consequences of our actions, humans are given an objective way of deciding what is right and wrong.

Some possible criticisms: Happiness is not the only thing of intrinsic worth as there is also love, human life and freedom. There is also doubt as to whether the ends do always justify the means and you are making moral decisions based on what may or may not happen in the future. Furthermore, the idea that you can assign a value to pleasure makes all pleasures comparable which is unrealistic, as is the idea that everyone feels happiness in the same way. There is also the notion that people are inherently selfish and will justify their actions as being in the interests of the many. What might be a popular belief felt by many, might not make it right. Actions can be deemed bad even if there happened to be no harmful consequences.

For further explanation and examples of applying utilitarianism access the Crash Course Philosophy at: **https://youtu.be/-a739VjqdSI?list=PLKcbSH9ZEFGSNL_ kd8Kd4b9CyFC1ZcTLs**

ACTIVITY: EXPLORING UTILITARIAN ETHICS

- Do you agree that something is morally right if it brings about happiness? (Consider whether morality and happiness are really the same thing.)

- Can you think of any examples of things that bring about happiness for large numbers of people but which might not seem morally correct?

- Can we measure happiness?

- Has Bentham missed anything from his criteria?

- Is Mill correct to argue that there are different levels of happiness?

- Are intellectual pleasures definitely better than 'animal' ones?

■ Situation ethics

Situation ethics is a consequentialist theory that became prominent in the 1960s through the work of Joseph Fletcher.

Christian notion of love – 'agape'

■ Situation ethics places the Christian notion of love – agape – at the heart of all moral decision-making which can differ depending on the situation. Therefore, the notion of absolute and universal moral laws is rejected.

■ Situation ethics distinguishes that what is morally right is often mistaken for the same as what is morally good.

■ Humans do not possess a separate faculty for a conscience that guides action, if conscience is defined by intuition or God speaking to people. Conscience is just the term used for taking the appropriate decisions according to the situation.

■ Actions do not have an inherent moral value – they are defined as moral by their consequences.

■ Situation ethics has four working principles and six fundamental principles in its structure.

Four working principles	Six fundamental principles
1 Pragmatism – for an action to be right then it must be effective. The end by which this success must be judged is 'agape'.	1 There is nothing good other than love. Helping people is good, hurting people is bad.
2 Relativism – Christians should not lay down any laws and reject words such as 'always' and 'never' as every case is different. However, everything must be relative to love.	2 Agape is the principle of love that does not expect love in return and replaces all laws and regulations. Placing love as the only principle calls people to higher level of responsibility.
3 Positivism – people come to faith voluntarily and situation ethics depends on this decision of free will to place love first. People have to see this for themselves and you cannot force them.	3 Love and justice are the same thing.

4	Personalism – people come first and not laws or principles.	4	Love wills good for the neighbour irrespective of whether you like them or not. Your neighbour could be your enemy.
		5	Only the end justifies the means and love really is the only end that should be sought.
		6	Love's decisions are made according to each situation. Moral laws only work theoretically and not in practice. People must be trusted with the freedom to make decisions based on agape alone.

Some possible strengths: Situation ethics is sensitive and respectful to circumstances, context and cultures and avoids what can be perceived as an overly rational, impersonal and scientific approach in other ethical frameworks.

It recognizes that moral decisions are unique to each particular situation and is based on the fundamental teaching that actions are right if they have the well-being of others as their objective. Overall, there is a flexibility of approach that reflects the reality of much moral decision-making.

Some possible criticisms: By treating every situation as different, it can seem like there is no ethical framework at all. Without some universality of ideas and rules, it compromises the notion of guaranteeing human rights and ignores a basic human desire to work within a framework of rules to manage human behaviour.

The notion of love is broad and hard to define, so it is hard to implement a system that lacks consistency and depends so much on a person only knowing the right course of action if they consider all the possible consequences and the people affected. It can be uncomfortable to work within a system of thinking that deems that murder and lying can be justified in specific situations.

ACTIVITY: EXPLORING SITUATION ETHICS

- Is it right that actions should be judged by their consequences?

- What does it mean for an action to be loving? How might love be defined?

- How might a supporter of situation ethics decide whether capital punishment was right and wrong?

- Where does conscience stand in this ethical framework?

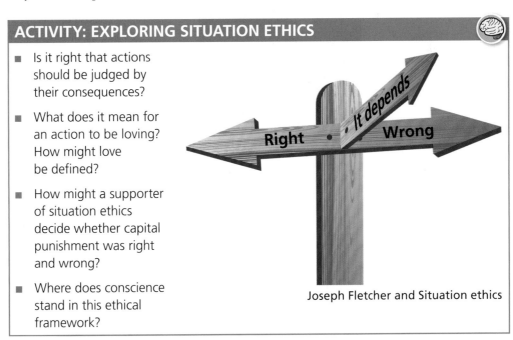

Joseph Fletcher and Situation ethics

Applied ethics

As applied ethics seeks the practical application of normative ethics to specific issues and situations, it is appropriate that you explore this area through a series of different activities.

ACTIVITY: APPLIED ETHICS

Look at the following thoughts, scenarios and dilemmas:

- Consider the Virtue, Kantian, Utilitarian and Situation ethics' response where applicable.

- Then think about your class' response as well as your own response.

- Would your response change when applied to a different context?

- It might help to visualize your findings in a mind map.

1 **Dilemma of torture**

2 **Killing in the context of Dietrich Bonhoeffer**

3a **Truth telling and The Inquiring Murderer:** Kant believed that it is always right to tell the truth. He gives the example of an axe murderer who asks you where their (innocent!) victim is.

> 'To tell a falsehood [lie] to a murderer who asked us whether our friend, of whom he was in pursuit, had not taken refuge in our house, would be a crime.'
>
> Immanuel Kant, *The Metaphysics of Morals*, 1785

3b What would be a Situation ethics response be to Kant's thoughts on lying?

> 'Since "circumstances alter cases", situationism holds that in practice what in some times and places we call right is in other times and places wrong… For example, lying is ordinarily not in the best interest of interpersonal communication and social integrity, but is justifiable nevertheless in certain situations.'
>
> Joseph Fletcher, 'Naturalism, situation ethics and value theory', in *Ethics at the Crossroads*, 1995

4 'The dilemma of prolonging life: "Imagine you are a doctor and you can choose either to prolong the life of an eighty-year-old woman for three years or to give hip transplants to six forty-year-old women who at present cannot walk. Which would you choose and why? Would your choice be different if the eighty-year old woman was your grandmother – if so, why?"

> Peter Vardy and Paul Grosch, *The Puzzle of Ethics*, 1994

5 **War:** During the Second World War there was a policy of bombing civilian targets (called 'area bombing') in the hope that the powers in question would be weakened by the loss of morale. As well as breaking down the ethical response to this, consider more contemporary contexts of war and whether the same reasoning would apply.

6 Look at the following definition of 'post-truth' which has become a popular adjective recently. What effect does this have on ethical reasoning and debate? Can you think of examples where this has been relevant?

Post-truth: relating to or denoting circumstances in which objective facts are less influential in shaping public opinion than appeals to emotion and personal belief.

Further sources for investigation:

- The similarities and differences between situation ethics and utilitarianism are explored in this video: **https://youtu.be/WgjIdswNP14**

- Peter Vardy and Paul Grosch discuss the nature of ethics in *The Puzzle of Ethics* – a guide to key philosophers as well as ethics deriving from specific religions and issues that raise ethical concerns for contemporary society.

- A good place to see the discussion of authentic ethical dilemmas and contemplate the different perspectives and ways people respond and act can be found at: **www.bbc. com/ideas/playlists/a-question-of-ethics**

ACTIVITY: CREATE YOUR OWN THEORY

Can you think of better ways to decide how to behave than these ethical theories? Consider as an individual the elements you most admire from the ethical theories discussed and then work with a peer or a group to create your own ethical theory. What is its main purpose? How should decisions be made? How does it take into account culture and society?

Present it to your class and discuss the similarities and differences in your responses. What conclusions can you come to about ethical theories and the questions they must ask and answer?

CHAPTER SUMMARY KEY POINTS

- Take time to understand the difference between meta-ethics, normative ethics and applied ethics and how they are significant in the work you are undertaking as well as the outside world.

- Ethical theories can give us a framework to explore the complexities of ethical dilemmas and work out where we stand.

- Considering the ethical dimension of a dilemma is not about what is right or wrong but about the multiple perspectives that can emerge.

- Ethical theories are centred around the person, the act or the consequence.

- To find your own voice, it is important to explore how you can apply different theories to different scenarios and the effect this has.

Formulating suitable

1. Find an issue relating to your career-related study.

→ 1. Bullying on social media sites.

2. Create a question that allows you to describe what you already know.

→ 2. How might harassment on the internet affect young people's self esteem?

3. Redraft this question so it asks for a solution.

→ 3. How has body shaming on social media platforms been tackled by its hosts?

4. Now try and think of the ethical dilemma that is actually in question. You have the issue but what is the element that presents differences of perspectives?

→ 4. Should there be harsher penalties for people who use social media platforms to body shame other users?

5. Now focus on the ethical dilemma and widen it so that the actual question goes beyond the limits of the original observation in step 2. Your question should prompt multiple suggestions as to the right answer and therefore require the use of argument.

→ 5. Should social media hosts such as Facebook do more to protect its teenage users from body-shaming abuse?

Checklist for a good question

The ethical issue is clear ☐

The dilemma is clear ☐

There is no bias implicit in the question ☐

The parameters of the question are not too broad ☐

The parameters of the question are not too specific ☐

The topic area is clearly relevant to the career-related subject ☐

Question starters that could lead to the right kind of title

Should X…?

Has X been successful?

Can X be justified?

Was X right to do Y?

Has X provided a beneficial effect?

The research question

Developing a research question

■ Why do I have to spend so much time on this?

Without the right question, there is a limit to how successful your reflective project can be. The question will provide you with the ethical and cultural framework or boundaries in which you are arguing. Get the question right and you will have a forum to explore ideas, debate strengths and weaknesses of ideas, and come to your own solutions. Get the question wrong and it will be like setting out for a run with just one shoe on. You might think it would be ideal if the perfect question just came to you in a moment of inspiration but actually working at getting the question right is an excellent exercise in critical thinking.

Criterion A

To gain the highest marks for Criterion A: Focus and Method you can see from the first bullet point here that you need to get the question right as it will set you up to achieve as highly as possible in your research.

■ Clear identification of an issue linked to the career-related study, and the arising ethical dilemma. The relevance of the study is clear. The research question is clearly stated and sharp focus on it is sustained throughout the project.

■ There is evidence of excellent planning of research, and the determination and collection of appropriate and varied sources. There is evidence of understanding of potential bias and source validity and measures have been taken to limit bias through source selection.

General advice

Building a research question raises many questions

■ It needs to be an evaluative question, which means there needs to be alternative viewpoints/interpretations that you can assess throughout rather than a purely descriptive or explanatory account.

■ The question should be clear in its relation to your career-related subject.

■ The question should suggest what will follow is a discussion and debate.

■ The ethical dilemma should be clear in your question. This means it should be evident that you are taking on a valid quandary where there is a range of valid perspectives to evaluate and not necessarily a clear moral solution.

■ Remember, ethical dilemmas also can be conflict of interest issues in the workplace and society.

■ A narrower title works and a broader one does not. The word limits for either Option 1 and 2 might seem a lot but you will need a tight focus.

■ There must be sufficient academic resources around your chosen title to sustain your research. The reflective project is 50 hours of your time so you need to ask yourself whether your title lends itself to this amount and depth of work.

■ How to avoid a question that leads to a descriptive reflective project

Descriptive projects, no matter how interesting, do not fulfil the requirements of the reflective project as they tend to lead to the pursuit of a single answer or just why something has happened. A good question promotes different viewpoints on a socially significant matter.

EXAMPLE TASK: QUESTION BUILDING AND BREAKDOWN

Student 1 is a Health and Social Care Student.

His initial question was 'How might harassment on the internet affect young people?'

What do you think? The student has clearly identified an ethical issue, which is great. However, the structure of this question will lead to descriptions of events and a conclusion rather than a debate of the issue. Furthermore, the context of the internet and young people is doubly vague and far too broad for a reflective project.

His first attempt at rephrasing led to: 'How is body shaming on the internet justified?'

Here is a question that might precede a debate and it is clear the focus has been narrowed down to an ethical issue. However, the ethical dilemma is not really here or in any balance as it presupposes that there might be a case for body shaming. Putting aside whether this is right or wrong, practically the student will find it hard to come up with credible sources to help them explore this.

Second attempt: 'Should there be harsher penalties for people who use social media platforms to body shame other users?'

This is better as you can almost anticipate the different perspectives that might emerge in the debate that follows. The ethical dilemma is clear – should people who abuse others be punished? There are clear ethical principles clashing here that make it a debate without an easy solution, such as the right to freedom of speech versus duty of care by corporations to protect users. The student will still have to be careful that they clearly set the parameters for the exact context they are researching, as well as how this issue is important to their career-related subject. They will also need to ensure they do not become descriptive when investigating the current penalties in place. One concern however is that while the word 'harsher' might seem needed to stop this dilemma becoming a little too broad, it is subjective and therefore bias is implicit in the title.

Final question: 'Should social media hosts such as Facebook do more to protect its teenage users from body-shaming abuse?'

This question has a clear ethical issue of online abuse and the quandary of whether social media platforms have a duty of care to protect their users. Interesting to place the word 'teenage' here as that narrows down the focus to a topical area; it might open up a connection to the career-related subject of health and social care. This final question also might be suitable with the right angle and possible tweak for a Business Studies essay.

Create a question step by step

Simple steps to a question

■ How to avoid a descriptive reflective project

This is developed in further detail in Chapter 6 on research methods, but there are five essential steps to developing a research question. We take the topic explored in detail in the Example Task and summarize how the question might be built using these steps.

1 Find an issue relating to your career-related study.

2 Create a question that allows you to describe what you already know.

How might harassment on the internet affect young people's self-esteem?

3 Redraft this question so it asks for a solution.

How has body shaming on social media platforms been tackled by its hosts?

4 Now try and think of the ethical dilemma that is actually in question. You have the issue but what is the element that presents differences of perspectives?

Should there be harsher penalties for people who use social media platforms to body shame other users?

5 Now focus on the ethical dilemma and widen it so that the actual question goes beyond the limits of the original observation in step 2. Your question should prompt multiple suggestions as to the right answer and therefore require the use of argument.

Should social media hosts such as Facebook do more to protect its teenage users from body-shaming abuse?

ACTIVITY: BECOME QUESTION EXPERTS

a   Consider the consequences for the reflective project for the following problems that have arisen with questions before:

- The ethical issue is not clear.

- The dilemma is not clear.

- There is bias implicit in the question.

- The parameters of the question are too broad.

- The parameters of the question are too specific

- The topic area is irrelevant to the career-related subject.

b   Consider the questions in the table below and evaluate how they are suitable for a reflective project.

Examples of issues	Research questions	Career-related subjects
Gender inequality in pay	Should men and women be paid equally in professional tennis?	Sport and Exercise Science
The decline of town centre shops due to online shopping	Should online businesses such as Amazon be morally obliged to help traditional small businesses?	Business Studies
Censorship of art	Is it right to censor some art?	Art and Design
Advancements in Artificial Intelligence	Should the development of AI be regulated?	Engineering
Data protection measures on the internet	Has the General Data Protection Regulation (GDPR) introduced in May 2018 improved privacy protection?	Information Technology
Increase in mental health decline in teenagers in 2018	Should schools make yoga and meditation compulsory to improve the mental health of teenagers?	Health and Social Care

CHAPTER SUMMARY KEY POINTS

- Creating the right research question is an essential and possibly lengthy process.

- Make sure you follow the five steps to a good research question.

- Be prepared to revisit these steps once you have embarked on research, as refining your question is an important part of your reflective journey.

- Ensure you use the advice on trouble shooting included in this chapter; look at as many examples of questions as possible and assess their strengths and weaknesses.

Critically examining

There are five main stages in the research process:

1. Defining the research's purpose and objectives and the research question.

2. Conducting a literature review.

3. Designing appropriate data collection methods and analysing the data.

4. Reflecting on the research methodology adopted.

5. Presenting the research findings to your supervisor.

research

Research skills you will need to use:	When you are reading, you could colour-code for:
Collect primary, secondary and tertiary research	The issue that contains your ethical dilemma
Differentiate between types of texts	Your ethical issue in context
Find interesting and original sources	Different perspectives that make this a dilemma
Read a text effectively	Cultural influences
Ask meaningful questions	Impact of the issue on different communities
Make notes that matter	Potential bias
Collect and analyse data	
Evaluate the bias	
Carry out a literature review	
Make connections between texts	
Synthesize information in your notes	
Recognize growth and gaps in knowledge	
Create a successful bibliography	

Research methods

LEARNER PROFILE ATTRIBUTES	
Principled	Inquirer
Balanced	Thinker

EXPERT TIP

At the end of every research session, no matter how short, ask yourself the question 'What do I think of this?' and make a note of any thoughts, questions or confusion that has arisen. This is an excellent way of taking an expert role in your project and finding your own voice.

Research methods and the importance of academic honesty

What are research methods? This is the process you go through to collect information and data in an academically honest way.

Making your knowledge, understanding and thinking completely visible throughout your reflective project is at the heart of keeping it academically honest. The marking criteria, as well as design of the project as a body of work with a separate reflection, make it clear that it is not just about what you know but how you have constructed your ideas and why you accept or reject certain perspectives. In a technological world that is constantly changing, the way we learn is also changing and it is hard to know how to use sources. By learning and applying research skills, you will not only see how knowledge is constructed, and the concepts and values that they hold, but also how you construct your own knowledge and find your own voice.

■ Understanding the process and the criteria

For your research you are going to 'select and explore an ethical dilemma embedded in an issue linked to a career-related context' and to do so you will 'select and apply appropriate research methods and collect and select relevant information from a variety of sources, showing an understanding of bias and validity' (Criterion A: Focus and Method). This process will help you develop critical thinking skills and 'demonstrate logical reasoning processes and the ability to interpret, analyse and evaluate material'. The more evidence you look at, the more you will 'develop the ability to synthesize information, making connections and linking ideas and evidence' (Criterion C: Critical Thinking). This will mean you will 'demonstrate knowledge and understanding of the issue' as well as 'contextualise the ethical dilemma and analyse different perspectives on it through the use of a local/global example of the issue in which the dilemma is embedded' (Criterion B: Knowledge and Understanding in context).

■ Role of the library, media or resource centre

The library and resource centre are essential

The library may already play a part in your day-to-day life at school or maybe you cannot remember when you last went there. Libraries differ from school to school but whatever the reality, the library and librarian are a vital resource in this process. The librarian (or other appropriately skilled teacher) is often asked to be part of the reflective project process as they have invaluable skills when it comes to helping students search for valid sources and introducing you to referencing and using citations accurately for the first time. A school will often have access to online databases and different periodicals and the librarian may well be able to arrange inter-library loans. Your teachers will also want to help you access a wider range of helpful sources from larger institutions. Local universities all over the world have shown that they are very open to helping reflective project students with their research and are impressed that you are undertaking this level of work at your stage of education.

Role of specialists in the community

Recognizing that there are people in your community who are already specialists in the issue you are exploring adds another dimension to your research. Interviewing someone is a rewarding way of gathering information and finding different perspectives, as well as an excellent opportunity to practise your questioning and communication skills. Maybe you have already identified someone you would like to interview in your service learning or this is the first time you have considered it. Take time to explore this option as it gives a real

Recognize the resources in your community

authenticity to your work in the way it connects directly to the community. There are activities in this book that will help you prepare thoughtful questions for interview.

The aim of the literature review

As you will see from the infographic on page 54, carrying out a literature review as soon as possible tells you early on whether your reflective project is going to work or not and gives you an opportunity to have a frank discussion about it with your supervisor. A racing driver wouldn't keep driving their car if they knew the tyres needed changing as there would be no hope of finishing, never mind winning the race; stopping and restarting might feel frustrating but do it quickly and the time can be made up.

Look at your sources critically and honestly

■ What goes in a literature review?

Once you have understood the requirements of the reflective project, narrowed down to a particular focus and arrived at a research question you are well into the process of the literature review already. The more you read, the more you will spot particular themes and perspectives emerging and the way different sources may or may not support these. To review your sources, it is not about going through each source individually and giving it a mark out of ten as that would be tedious. However, using a thematic approach, such as taking certain perspectives, stakeholders, cultures or communities that have struck you as interesting, and using tools to analyse where sources are relevant and how far they might support a certain theme will help you greatly. You can ascertain if you lack credible sources in particular areas or in the whole research area or you might also start to see how your whole structure might unfurl. Use the suggestions in this chapter to help you carry out your literature review. There is an exercise that can help you carry out a literature review with your supervisor on page 73.

■ What to do with a disappointing literature review

If you have a question in mind but have found limited or just too many sources or ideas surrounding it, this is the time to stop and revise your focus. This might feel disappointing but proceeding with a question that you know deep down does not really work will set you up for a frustrating and difficult time. Your work is not wasted as changing direction and adapting is a crucial part of reflection. It may be that you can refine or refocus your search area just a little to get the question on the right track.

■ Read around the topic

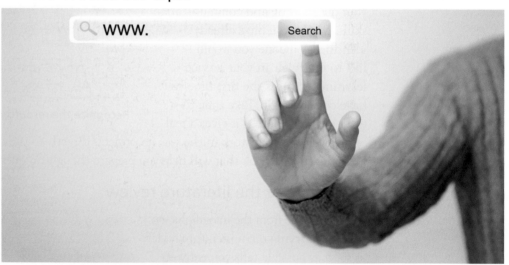

The internet is just one source

Start by reading articles, newspapers, magazines, books and websites that will not only deepen your knowledge of your chosen issue but will get you used to handling different types of sources and seeing what is out there. What you read at this stage will help you confirm the ethical dilemma you are focusing on and create a good interrogative question which you can discuss with your supervisor.

■ Understand implications of source type

Keep in mind that a big internet search engine might seem accessible but sources are not listed necessarily by the quality of the literature. Big search engines such as Google also have academic areas, for example **www.googlescholar.com**, but these take time to get used to. More specifically, academic databases might give you relevant and credible sources but the language can take time to get used to and feel difficult to get through. Read on through this chapter to find out how to ask the right questions about sources.

■ What is the difference between primary, secondary and tertiary research?

Actually, the process starts in reverse with **tertiary research**! These sources synthesize information gathered from other sources and are often in an easily accessible and concise form. Tertiary sources include encyclopaedias, chronologies and textbooks. They are good for an overview and finding out some of the key words at play but not for getting to the heart of an issue. However, do look at the bibliographies that accompany them as you may find names of experts you would like to explore later.

The research you may be most familiar with is the use of **secondary sources** as you have probably already read some journal or newspaper articles in preparation. These texts analyse, review or restate information in primary resources or other secondary sources. Examples include biographies, scholarly articles, review articles, historical studies or literature reviews. However, you need to be aware that secondary sources vary greatly in quality; see below for tips on how to test how good a source is.

Primary research is research conducted by someone directly. You can use primary research someone else has created or conduct your own primary research. Types of primary research might vary more than your think. Scientific primary research means data sets, technical reports or experimental research results. However, it is prominent in other areas too as primary sources could involve diaries, narratives, autobiographies, memoirs, speeches, novels, plays, poems, works of art and popular culture.

■ Potential useful data

In philosophy, data can mean things known or assumed as facts, making the basis of reasoning or calculation.

As you can see from the definition, data does not just mean numbers, graphs and charts in the form of statistics. It also means information and facts, and these can come from multiple places and not just essays, books or articles, as shown in the examples below:

- An interview with an expert on your issue in question that has been published in an online or print form.

- An interview that you have conducted yourself with a reputable authority.

- Statistics from credible government, non-government and professional organizations.

- Documentaries.

- Internet sites from reputable authorities such as universities, museums and non-governmental organizations.

DEFINITIONS

Data

1   facts and statistics collected together for reference or analysis

Synonyms: facts, figures, statistics

Do you know what data means?

Primary and secondary research pitfalls:

- Avoid using yourself as a primary source. This is not allowed.

- Avoid leaving data unanalysed or allocated to the appendices. Make sure you use the data you find. This might sound obvious but the information you collect should back up and synthesize with your ideas in your main essay. Examiners are not obliged to read the appendices so do not put anything important to your main analysis in there.

- Avoid using long quotes. More importantly, avoid using long quotes and then not analysing them. This is really just copying and plagiarism software will pick up on it.

- Avoid conducting small surveys where you ask your classmates, or immediate community, a few questions. Although this can be good for gaining an insight into some initial perspectives, it is not proof enough to add any sense of depth or weight to your main argument.

■ Producing your own primary research

To produce your own data, it must be scientifically valid, which means it must be conducted on a convincing scale and be representative of the community you are studying. If you would like to carry out your own primary research then consider the following tips to help you succeed:

- First, decide what is the purpose of carrying out your own primary research and that your own research is absolutely necessary to the issue and dilemma you are exploring.

- Work out who you will ask, what you will ask them and why you will ask them.

- Make the questions count; take time to create the questions using the Socratic method detailed in Chapter 7.

Using the internet as a source

You will undoubtedly not remember a life without the internet like your teachers can. It is hugely powerful and you will use it, but you must use it well. Luckily, there has been plenty of advice out there for a long time on how to use internet sources effectively and honestly. Remember that anyone can say anything at anytime from anywhere in the world on the internet irrespective of its truth.

- Avoid relying on internet searches and ignoring other key sources.

- Avoid taking sources at face value and not critically evaluating the quality of the information.

- Avoid copying information from the internet and not acknowledging your sources.

Be an internet detective

Questions to ask of internet sources:

- Who? Question the source of information

- What? Question the content of information

- Where? Question the location of the information

Source: Adapted from 'The Internet Detective' – a free online critical thinking tutorial that was developed by the University of Bristol and Manchester Metropolitan University in 2006.

ACTIVITY: THE INTERNET DETECTIVE

Look for clues. Using two to three sources you have identified as potentially useful, assess their quality using the following markers:

- **Research evidence** – there should be signs of research methods, data and other reviewed sources in their work.

- **Proper references** – it is not enough to have citations and references; they must be from respected sources and good quality.

- **Mistakes and inaccuracies** – errors might point towards a source that has not been checked or properly edited. This could be a warning sign.

- **Dates** – when citing internet sources you must put the date that you accessed it in your bibliography. However, you need to check when your source was written, published and last updated as it might seem hugely useful for your research topic but out-of-date in relation to recent developments.

- **Bias and controversial statements that are unsubstantiated** – trust your instinct; if you suspect it does not add up and goes against your own knowledge you have collated so far then look for signs of bias.

There is more on spotting bias in the following pages.

■ Activities to promote successful research

■ Critically examine your research from the very beginning

Research needs critical examination

As you start to read, remember you are in charge. Have a simple colour-coding process for key areas you are looking for as suggested on page 55, and write down any key words, phrases or ideas that might be helpful in future research and/or relate to the reflective project guidelines. You will need to assess every source for bias. Take time to reflect in your RRS about the literature you have uncovered. See tips and activities in this chapter to help you with this reflection before you present your literature review to your supervisor.

Reading for critical analysis

ACTIVITY: SCAN READING

First, you will want to work out if a source will be useful and this can be done quicker than you think.

- First, flick through – scanning.

- Look at the index.

- Look at the headlines.

- Look at the pictures.

- Look at any summaries at the beginning or end of chapters.

- Stop and glance at anything that interests you.

- Jot down anything you already know – key words.

- Produce a mind map to develop ideas further.

- Always make notes and ask yourself questions.

- Don't forget the colour-coding.

■ Finding interesting, diverse and useful sources, and identifying validity and bias

As you look at sources more deeply, you need to interrogate the author and ask questions as you are reading. The suggested questions will help make you more of an active reader and might give you more confidence in how to use a text.

- How do I know this is true?

- If it is true, what else follows?

Interrogate the text

- Is the conclusion justified? How do I know?

- What is being presumed or assumed here?

- Is this fact or opinion and what evidence do I have?

- If it's fact, is it always true? If it's opinion, can I trust the source?

- Are there any (better) examples to illustrate the argument?

- Is this logical?

- What is my personal opinion and has it changed? Can it be justified?

- What new points have been made for my topic?

- What is essential to know and what is just padding?

■ A closer look at keywords

Contextualize – this means to analyse a word or event in terms of the words or concepts surrounding it.

The issue you have chosen is not in isolation; by considering local, global and cultural influences currently connected to it, you are contextualizing it.

Synthesize – to combine ideas from a range of sources in order to group and present common ideas or arguments, as well as develop and strengthen your own arguments.

Once you have read a range of sources, you will start to notice ideas that connect in some ways and this is when you can start to synthesize this information.

■ Recognizing growth and gaps in knowledge and understanding

You will need to maintain the same level of focus on your dilemma in your research as you will in your writing. It is important to organize your ideas as you go so you can start to see your arguments emerging as well as spot where you need more help.

- Keep to the topic at all times and keep going back to your question.

- Gather together all the research you have done – notes from books, sources from the internet. When you have your notes together try mind mapping the key ideas.

- Now start to add to the mind map, putting ideas together in groups and consider how they connect.

Have you considered local and global influences?

- Check – are your points focused on the question or even suggesting a solution?

- Check – have you considered the significance of local, global and cultural influences?

- You might be able to see your introduction, middle and ending emerging already.

■ Recognizing bias

Can you recognize a trustworthy source?

This is an important skill when researching for the reflective project as it depends on assessing the strengths and weaknesses of multiple perspectives. You will be dealing with opinions that might show a leaning towards a particular viewpoint but if it is prejudice or seems unfair then that is a bias that you must take into account.

ACTIVITY: KNOW YOUR BIAS

To start, can you tell the difference between fact, opinion or speculation?

What is the difference between factual, opinion or speculative claims?

Look at the following claims and divide them up between fact (even if you do not believe them!), opinion or speculation:

- Germany's population is currently 52 million.

- It is morally wrong to go to war.

- More boys do STEM subjects at university than girls.

- 3.6 billion TV viewers watched at least one minute of the Rio 2016 Olympics.

- If we do not ban migration soon, the country will be full.

- It is possible to do the IBCP at my school.

- Brexit will mean that the UK economy is depressed for years.

Now discuss how you would assess the reliability of each of the claims.

What would you need to do to verify the factual claims?

How would you assess the opinions and speculative claims?

■ Assessing the credibility of sources

Here's a way of building on your understanding of bias and assessing the reliability of a source as well as developing your critical thinking; use the mnemonic RAVEN:

Remember to use RAVEN

Reputation – The reputation of the publication/author. How might this affect, positively or negatively, the reliability of the source? Has the source been reliable in the past or has it distorted the truth?

Ability to see – Is it a primary or secondary source? Is the author, or their own sources, in a position to know what they are talking about?

Vested interest – Does the source have a 'hidden agenda' in presenting one side of the argument as more compelling than the other? Do they have anything at stake personally or professionally in the issue?

Expertise – What are the author/publication's credentials? Are they an expert in the field on which they are writing? Have they used expert witnesses?

Neutrality – Is there any reason to suspect bias? For example, newspapers have a 'leaning' towards a political stance.

Source: adapted from R Brink-Budgen and J Thawaites (2012) *OCR AS Critical Thinking*. Deddington: Philip Allan Updates.

ACTIVITY: CREDIBILITY OF SOURCES

Now look at a source you have chosen using RAVEN:

- What is it claiming?

- What information are you using from it?

- Is it fact, opinion or speculation?

- How did you make this judgment?

- If it is factual, how do you check the accuracy of the facts given?

- If it is opinion or speculation, how reliable is it and why?

ACTIVITY: THE QUADRANT LITERATURE REVIEW

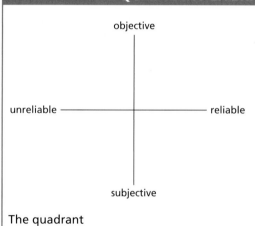

The quadrant

Using 'The quadrant' is a good way of evaluating the strengths and weaknesses of your sources and deciding where you might need more information. Draw the quadrant on a piece of large paper for your RRS and consider each of the sources you have used so far: look at how relevant they are to your topic and their reliability using the criteria in this chapter. This will give you an overview of your work as you go along and inform your next steps. You could project the quadrant onto a screen or wall and use sticky notes with your sources on them so you can move ideas around and make decisions about which sources to remove - this is a great discussion to have with your supervisor. Remember to take a photo for your RRS.

EXPERT TIP

The labels for the axes on the quadrant diagram are just suggestions for this exercise but you can decide other parameters to judge the sources by. For example, you could use it for exploring bias, sides of arguments, fact and opinion, or assessing the strengths and weaknesses of questions.

The source for this exercise is adapted from visible thinking tools on **www.pz.harvard.edu**

REFLECTION POINT

Using the RRS for reflection on research so far. You will want to gather your thoughts as you complete your first full reflection in the RPPF.

Questions you might have	RRS tools you might use
What have I learned so far?	Colour-coded notes
How have my initial questions changed?	Original mind map of questions with your annotated responses
What obstacles have I faced?	A recorded conversation with your supervisor where you discuss any problems you are having and the different perspectives that are emerging from your research
Now that I have done some initial reading, is my research question appropriate? Is my research question allowing me to be critical or is it leading me to be descriptive?	A reflection from a conversation with your supervisor
Is my research question suitable for 3 000 words?	A mindmap applying the infographic on pages 48–49

ACTIVITY: RESEARCH SKILLS PRESENTATION

Working with a partner or a small group, see how much you have understood about research. Below are research skills discussed in this chapter that you will need in this research process. Discuss all of them together and make a poster with tips on how to be successful in three to five of the skills you think are the most important.

- Collect primary, secondary and tertiary research

- Differentiate between types of texts

- Find interesting and original sources

- Read a text effectively

- Ask meaningful questions

- Make notes that matter

- Collect and analyse data

- Evaluate the bias

- Carry out a literature review

- Make connections between texts

- Use sources to contextualize an issue

- Synthesize information in your notes

- Recognize growth and gaps in knowledge

CHAPTER SUMMARY KEY POINTS

- Read and re-read the assessment criteria and academic honesty definition throughout the process and remind yourself that the key to being academically honest is to keep visible, at all times, where you obtained information and ideas from, in your notes and writing.

- Select an issue that interests you from a bank of possible ideas. Ask yourself 'what will be the purpose of my research?'

- Carry out a literature review: read around your chosen issue to gauge whether there are interesting and useful sources out there that will help you formulate a question with an ethical dilemma. Present your findings to your supervisor before completing your RPPF.

- If you have a question in mind but have found a disappointing amount of sources or ideas surrounding it, change it now and stop. This might feel frustrating but it is a fraction of the frustration you will feel if you carry on now with a weak question.

- Now you have a question, plan HOW you will investigate and produce your reflective project. Set yourself specific objectives for your research so you remain feeling in control. You are becoming the expert here.

- Plan an initial structure that is based on the research you have done and supports the research question; this may simply be a two to three areas that support a certain perspective you have noticed plus an area for a counter-argument. This structure may well change and become more complex the more research you do but it will help you approach sources with more confidence.

- Carry out the research in an active, analytical and engaged way. The key words here are variety and quality. Do not rely on one type of source altogether – journals, books and databases are just some you could use.

- Remember, you are not just carrying out research – you are critically examining this research as well throughout the process and not just in your writing. Look over your research and highlight the different perspectives. Take time to make notes of your own thoughts on the different perspectives as you go along as this analysis will help you in the writing process and is an essential part of your reflective process.

- It is far easier and helpful to collate all the research sources you have used as you go along and place them in a bibliography to be included in their final submission. Remember, a crucial part of the RPPF is to reflect on how you carried out your research with a reflection on the successes and problems you may have encountered and how you responded. Discussions with your supervisor will help you shape your ideas here.

- Are you ready to start writing? In your RRS, reflect in a mind map on what you need to do before starting the drafting process. Do you need to revisit any of the steps so far?

A supervisor should:

Know the official regulations and criteria for the reflective project

Encourage you to reflect on the challenges you come across

Push you to ask the right questions

Be a source of advice, encouragement and a sounding board for your ideas

Give you feedback on your first draft in accordance with the criteria

Conduct three official meetings to inform your three reflections in your RPPF

Officially, check you are keeping on top of the process

Officially, ensure you are carrying out your work in an academically honest and ethical way

Officially, verify you have done so in the final submission of your work to the IB and fill out a supervisor's report

the supervisor

A
student
should:

Take ownership of the process and be proactive at all times

Keep all research academically honest

Keep to meeting times

Refer consistently to the criteria

Stick to a timeline and deadlines sent

Go to meetings prepared with the RRS and questions

Not be chased at any point

The role of the supervisor

LEARNER PROFILE ATTRIBUTES	
Risk-taker	Communicator

Supervisors' and students' responsibilities

Use the time well with your supervisor

The reflective project is a major piece of independent learning and the final product must reflect that. However, it is a really important requirement of the reflective project that you receive three to five hours of individual support from a supervisor. This time allocation might include informal discussion but it also includes three formal meetings that will assist your completion of the three RPPF sections, as well as to give you feedback on your first draft. Having a communicative, open-minded and inquisitive attitude from the very start will ensure that the relationship you forge with your supervisor will be respectful and purposeful.

Common misconceptions about the supervisor:

- They will be an expert in your subject and specific issue; no – this is not their role.

- They will tell you what to do at every stage; no – they will encourage you to decide the next steps.

- They will mark multiple drafts; no – they will give feedback on just one.

- They will help you with your spelling and grammar; no – they are there to offer feedback on the criteria only.

- They do not mark your final essay; yes they do and they submit this to the IB assisted by the reflective project coordinator.

- They have no official sway; yes they do as they must verify the authenticity of your work and absolutely will report any over-assistance or malpractice such as plagiarism to your school and the IB.

A supervisor should:

- know the official regulations and criteria for the reflective project
- push you to ask the right questions
- encourage you to reflect on the challenges you come across
- be a source of advice, encouragement and a sounding board for your ideas
- give you feedback on your first draft in accordance with the criteria
- conduct three official meetings to inform your three reflections in your RPPF
- officially, check you are keeping on top of the process
- officially, ensure you are carrying out your work in an academically honest and ethical way
- officially, verify you have done so in the final submission of your work to the IB and fill out a supervisor's report.

A student should:

- take ownership of the process and be proactive at all times
- keep all research academically honest
- keep to meeting times
- refer consistently to the criteria
- stick to a timeline and deadlines sent
- go to meetings prepared with the RRS and questions
- not be chased at any point.

Go prepared to your supervisory meetings

ACTIVITY: SUGGESTIONS FOR MEETINGS

Be the expert from the beginning and be prepared for your supervisory session. Use your RRS to show your progress to your supervisor. You can revisit many of the suggestions below throughout the process but you should aim to use them at least once.

1	Go through the criteria together and discuss any worries or confusion you might have. Make sure you discuss 'academic honesty' and 'intellectual property'.
2	Discuss your understanding of ethical issues and dilemmas.
3	Introduce your supervisor to the Who, What, Why, When and Where of your chosen topic as far as you know at present.
4	Test the effectiveness of your question together using the tips in Chapter 5 The Research Question.
5	Discuss sources with your supervisor using the tips in Chapter 6 Research Methods.
6	Look at exemplars your supervisor will have access to.
7	Look also at The Reflective Project Guide, the Reflective Project Additional Guide and the IB publication *Effective citing and referencing*.

■ Collaborative activities for supervisor and student meetings
■ The start of the process

ACTIVITY: DISCUSSION FORUM

Early on in the process, organize a forum to discuss current topics and general debates within your career-related subject inviting your teachers, supervisors and any relevant stakeholders (other students, parents, governors, community members) you think would contribute well to the discussion. This is not to discuss individual reflective projects. You might start by discussing the difference between an issue and a dilemma as many people find this distinction difficult no matter who they are.

> # The wisdom begins in wonder.
> - Socrates

Discuss using Socratic questioning

■ Questioning for discussion and your first draft

You have already been asking questions of the issue and dilemma you are researching, but your supervisor's questions in discussion can really help develop your understanding. They might employ the 'Socratic questioning' model which contains six types of questions. You can also use this when checking your work.

1 Questions for clarification

   Why do you say that?

   How does this relate to our discussion?

2 Questions that probe assumptions

   What is being assumed here?

   How can you verify or disapprove that assumption?

3 Questions that probe reason and evidence

   What might be an example?

   What is . . . analogous to?

   What do you think causes this to happen? Why?

4 Questions about viewpoints and perspectives

   What would be an alternative viewpoint?

   What is another way to look at it?

   Would you explain why it is necessary or beneficial, and who benefits?

   Why is . . . the best?

   What are the strengths and weaknesses of . . . ?

   How are . . . and . . . similar?

   What is a counterargument for . . . ?

5 Questions that probe implications and consequences

   What generalizations can you make?

   What are the consequences of that assumption?

   What are you implying?

   How does . . . affect . . . ?

   How does . . . tie in with what you have said before?

6 Questions about questions

What was the point of this question?

Why do you think I asked this question?

How does . . . apply to everyday life/different cultures/global and local context?

ACTIVITY: VISUALIZE YOUR LITERATURE REVIEW

objective

unreliable —————————————— reliable

subjective

Use the quadrant to discuss sources as suggested on page 65

You might have used this exercise in your research already. However, by talking it through with your supervisor, it will allow them to offer advice on the methods you are using and help you solve problems.

Using 'The quadrant' is a good way to remind you of evaluating the strengths and weaknesses of your sources and deciding where you might need more information. Draw the quadrant on a piece of large paper for your RRS and consider each of the sources you have used so far for how relevant they are to your topic and how reliable they are using the criteria discussed in this chapter. This will give you an overview of your work as you go along and inform your next steps. Remember, you could project the quadrant onto a screen or wall and use sticky notes with your sources on them so you can move ideas around and make decisions about which sources to remove. Record your findings for your RRS.

EXPERT TIP

The labels for the axes on the quadrant diagram are just suggestions for this exercise but you can decide other parameters to judge the sources by. For example, you could use it for exploring bias, sides of arguments, fact and opinion, or assessing the strengths and weaknesses of questions.

■ Giving advice on the first draft

Feedback is a crucial point in the reflective project journey

Your supervisor needs to tread a fine line when giving you feedback to help improve your work before final submission. Too little feedback and you will not have constructive suggestions on how to progress but giving you too much feedback would defeat the purpose of this being a project about independent learning. Make sure you give your supervisor plenty of time to read your first draft and organize their thoughts before having a meeting to receive feedback.

What a supervisor cannot do with a student's work:

- Correct or rewrite any spelling, punctuation, grammar or information of any kind.
- Rewrite any part of the reflective project.
- Indicate where big structural changes might take place.
- Proofread the final draft for errors.
- Correct any citations or bibliographies.

What a supervisor can do with your draft of the reflective project is make observations and ask questions that will lead you to make your own inquiries and problem solve.

During your feedback discussion, your supervisor can advise you on HOW to improve on your reflective project by asking open questions but not specifically WHAT to change or edit in any way. The next full copy of your reflective project your supervisor will see is your final draft.

Possible open questions and comments your supervisor might use:

- Do you notice anything here?
- Could you make this clearer?
- What are you missing here?
- Could this belong elsewhere?
- Have you a voice?
- Check for consistency here.
- Check the accuracy here.
- Check you are are meeting requirements here for citations/bibliographies/appendices.
- Check you have answered all your questions and included all your relevant research.

Use open questions to help you both check your work

These open questions could prompt you to check:

- if your question has stayed the same throughout.

- if you have understood the full ethical impact of a perspective or idea.

- if you have constructed your analysis using REAL and SEAL (see Chapter 8).

- if you have included useful information in an appendix that belongs in the main work.

- if your argument is unbalanced.

- if your conclusion does not take into account the all the arguments you have put forward.

- if you have included your own ideas and offered possible solutions to your dilemma.

CHAPTER SUMMARY KEY POINTS

- Take ownership of the project and arrange meetings with your supervisor.

- Your supervisor will give you 3–5 hours of time including formal reflection sessions.

- Your supervisor will read and provide you with feedback on how the criteria were met in the first (and only) draft of your whole reflective project but will not edit it.

- Your supervisor will have access to exemplars and other useful IB documents to consult together.

- You should go prepared to your sessions with your RRS and questions you have.

- Your supervisor will mark and authenticate your project and the RPPF and submit the marks they have awarded you.

> 'I KEEP six honest serving-men (They taught me all I knew);
> Their names are What and Why and When and How and
> Where and Who'.
>
> *Rudyard Kipling*

Critical thinking tips

Don't accept things at face value

Ask probing questions

Use evidence to back up your arguments and different perspectives

Question if something might be true

Question the validity of a source or perspective

Assess all the evidence presented to offer solutions in a conclusion

thinking

Critical thinking phrases

Structure your ideas with the following discursive markers:

On the one hand …

On the other hand …

However …

Despite this …

Nevertheless …

The most significant point …

In the short term … but in the longer term …

The most convincing argument …

Critical thinking and writing the first draft

LEARNER PROFILE ATTRIBUTES	
Balanced	Risk-taker

What is critical thinking?

Critical thinking and analysis can sound daunting and serious but it is far from that; it is all about being able to question in a deep and effective way. It is also about being engaged, curious and open-minded about new ideas. Throughout your course so far, you have been taking part in critical thinking in all sorts of ways.

EXAMPLE TASK: CRITICAL THINKING IN THE CP

Look at the following statements and think of times when you demonstrated these.
- I ask important and probing questions.
- I don't just take things at face value and will question whether something might be true.
- I find evidence to substantiate my ideas and perspectives.
- I can assess evidence and come to conclusions.
- I can collaborate and communicate with others to find solutions to complex problems.
- I am open-minded to alternative ways of thinking and can assess their strengths and weaknesses.
- I can discuss assumptions, implications and consequences of different ways of thinking.

■ The significance of stakeholders in critical analysis

Interviewing interesting people can show critical thinking in action

The best way of understanding ethical, critical and reflective thinking is seeing it in action in an authentic way, as it is happening around you all the time, particularly in a professional setting. Earlier in this book, we discussed how interviewing interesting people from different professions is of fantastic benefit to the CP student for all sorts of reasons and not just for the reflective project.

On the left-hand side of the table below you can see the key phrases for achieving the highest marks in Criteria B, C and E. On the right-hand side, you can see key words taken from these phrases. They are all skills that can be appreciated and developed through the process of interview.

B: KNOWLEDGE AND UNDERSTANDING of ethical dilemma (7–9 marks)	
The central ethical dilemma is analysed from different perspectives …	Different perspectives
Developed knowledge and understanding …	Developed knowledge
The use of a local or global example is effective and well integrated …	Local and global examples
The impact of the ethical dilemma …	Ethical impact
Analysis of how cultural perspectives can influence …	Cultural perspectives

C: CRITICAL THINKING of ethical dilemma and evidence (9–12 marks)	
Considered and convincing discussion …	Convincing discussion
Interpreting and applying evidence …	Interpretation
Conclusions are perceptive and concise …	Perceptive conclusions
Connections made between ideas are insightful, sustained and coherent	Sustained connections

E: ENGAGEMENT AND REFLECTION of the project in the RPPF (5–6 marks)	
Evaluative …	Evaluative
The capacity to consider actions and ideas in response to setbacks …	Setbacks
Intellectual and personal engagement …	Intellectual engagement
Authenticity, intellectual initiative and/or creativity in the student voice…	Authenticity, initiative, creativity

ACTIVITY: BUILD YOUR OWN PROFESSIONAL NETWORK

In Chapter 2, it was suggested that you interview a professional, testing out some of the reflective questions you had created. Now you are further through the process, you can expand on your questions and the amount of people you interview to consider more of the higher order skills in the reflective project criteria as detailed above. The table below shows a list of possible interview topics that you could use.

INTERVIEW TOPICS
Education & career path
Ethical considerations
Intercultural understanding
Successes & setbacks
The Learner Profile's significance
Importance of Lifelong learning

This process helps you to see the role reflection has in a professional setting and is also an essential part of your PPS course. Creating and recording your own network across a range of professions will help you see the learner profile in action and how transferable skills can be.

■ Use your RRS to prepare for critical writing

Use your RRS to prepare for critical writing

ACTIVITY: STOCK TAKE YOUR RESEARCH

Before you start writing, look back on your RRS and identify where the strengths and weaknesses are in your research so far. The following table will help you do this and also suggests critical thinking tools you might use to help you fill specific gaps. Once you have done an audit of your research ask yourself 'Do I have any questions I have not resolved? Am I keeping to the schedule?'

Questions you might ask	Critical thinking reflective tools you might use
Do I have enough data and information to formulate my argument?	Stock-take your research: colour-code your notes and collated quotes for relevant perspectives and data that connect or conflict
If I do not have enough information, what should I do?	Write a draft introduction to your reflective project. (See below for details.)
How does the research I have gathered relate or conflict with my question?	Annotate this introduction to your reflective project to reflect on how clear your argument using REAL and SEAL (See below for details.)
Is the evidence collected suggesting I need to change my question?	Show your reworking of your research question.
Has my research taken me in any unexpected directions and how am I responding to this?	Annotate your data for how it is credible and relevant for your question.

■ Critical thinking activities

ACTIVITY: CHALLENGING ASSUMPTIONS

Find an advert that makes claims; for example, a car advert, which can often be conceptual in design.

In groups, discuss:

1 What is being advertised?

2 Who is the advert aimed at? Do you all agree?

3 What is being assumed about the intended audience?

4 What claims does the advert make? Do you trust it? Why?

5 What questions would you need to ask to check the claims are true?

6 Where could you find the answers?

7 Does the advert have smallprint and what is it used for?

8 What are the implications and consequences of the smallprint?

9 What are your conclusions about the advert's claims? Do you trust it?

10 What do others think and does this affect your perspective?

Just by having this discussion you are engaging in critical thinking. Look back at the definition at the start of the chapter and see how many skills you employed during this exercise.

Try to be balanced

■ Disagreeing with viewpoints and using counter-arguments

In the context of the reflective project, being balanced might mean having to address valid counter-arguments and different relevant perspectives that you might strongly disagree with. Placing yourself in someone else's position does not mean you are agreeing with them; it is showing that you can critically, rationally and, most of all, fairly break down the key arguments at play in your reflective project. You can only truly reject another perspective if you show you fully understand it.

ACTIVITY: PRACTISE COUNTER-ARGUING

Considering other points of view in detail is easier than you think. The purpose of this 10-minute activity is to argue what you do not believe. Take one of the following topics and state your opinion. Now try to create the strongest argument possible for what you do not believe. This will make you put yourself in their shoes and empathize.

Animal testing   Global warming   Capital punishment

EXPERT TIP

Is your counter-argument becoming stronger than your original case?

It is a fundamental part of the reflective project that you reflect on the way your research and critical analysis might challenge and change your thinking. If you find that your counter-argument is stronger than your original arguments, embrace it! Then review and rewrite your plan in your RRS to accommodate it. Do not forget to include this development in your RPPF.

■ The hesitant critical writer

You might be someone who struggles to start writing or feels a bit intimidated by the task ahead as you feel critical writing is not your strength. Starting is a question of risk-taking and not pressurising yourself to write perfectly. The following activity can be excellent for shaping your argument in your introduction as well as demonstrating critical thinking.

ACTIVITY: FINDING THE STORY

First, discuss the photo below, then try it yourself by finding an image that represents your reflective project's issue and dilemma.

2013 winner of World Press Photo of the Year

- What is the story?
- What is the untold story?
- What is your story?
- What is his/her story?
- What is our story?
- What is the bigger story?
- What is the smaller story?
- What is the scientific/historical/cultural story?

Reflection: What does each of these questions make you consider?

Adapted from critical thinking tools available at www.pz.harvard.edu

■ Finding your independent critical voice

ACTIVITY: THE COURTROOM DRAMA

You might be struggling to find where you stand personally in response to your issue and dilemma and be overwhelmed by different perspectives. A way of organizing your own thoughts in response to other perspectives is to visualize it and bring it to life. Try your question as a courtroom drama. Create a brief for yourself to establish what the issue is, as well as briefs for each stakeholder in your dilemma. Call forward these 'witnesses' and open it out to the class to ask questions of each one, testing their ideas. Close the proceedings as the judge putting forward your judgment on the debate. Make sure you reflect on this exercise in your RRS.

■ Starting writing

COMMON MISTAKE

- Avoid using the terms 'for' or 'against' in your contents page as it will give the impressin you are just discussing 'right' and 'wrong' and not a multi-dimensional issue.

■ The introduction

Remember that you have completed a literature review, which will help you contextualize your ethical dilemma and research question in the opening section. It is here that you are stating why your issue and dilemma is of importance and shaping the parameters under which your study will take place, so you must establish the local, global and cultural contexts and their significance. Most importantly, you must elaborate on the significance of this issue and dilemma in relation to your career-related study.

■ Structuring the main body of your writing

As you have been demonstrating through the process so far, critical thinking is all about the development of ideas and their evaluation. Look at the infographic at the start of this chapter for useful phrases to structure your essay. However, many students struggle with how to evaluate effectively. You are probably asked to 'evaluate' in some way in all of your subjects and with a term that is used so much, admitting that you find this hard might feel impossible – it is even harder to act on when you do not know where to start. The following suggestions of REAL and SEAL will build your initial ideas into complex points that consider the strengths and weaknesses of arguments and the impact on the community. You can use it during the research phase in a messy mind map or formally in your writing.

Structure and scaffold your paragraphs

Developing Ideas – REAL	Analysis and Evaluation – SEAL
Reason or idea	**S**tate strength and weaknesses in idea/reason/opinion
Evidence to support your idea	**E**xplain why it shows a strength or weakness
Analysis of how your example supports your reason or idea	**A**ssess the significance of this: what is the impact of this to the community and your argument?
Link with the focus of your project AND with other reasons or examples you have found	**L**ink to your previous points and/or to your next point

ACTIVITY: EXAMPLES OF CRITICAL WRITING

In the following examples from a student's reflective project, use the reflective project criteria to assess them and discuss the prompt question. Overall, what do you think the student is doing well? What could be missing? (Remember these are excerpts.) Think about Question, Research, Ethical and Critical Understanding, Communication and Student Voice.

How has this writer established the parameters of their reflective project?

Introduction

Cultural appropriation occurs when someone adopts elements from another culture without requesting the permission of the people from that culture. For example, Susan Scafidi, author of 'Who Owns Culture? Appropriation and Authenticity in the American Law', defines cultural appropriation as 'taking intellectual property, traditional knowledge, cultural expressions, or artefacts from someone else's culture without permission.'

An example of cultural appropriation happened in 2012 when an American retail company called Urban Outfitters copied the sacred Navajo tribal symbol and used it as their own design... This was offensive towards the Navajo Nation, as the Urban Outfitters product was a non-Native American product.

At the moment I'm currently studying Art & Design as my core subject for the Careers Program and I am very interested in the debate about cultural appropriation within the fashion industry. I chose this topic because it is linked to my BTEC qualification. On the other hand, I was interested to learn about cultural appropriation because I had heard a lot about it in the news prior to this project. This topic 'cultural appropriation' also has a lot of moral dilemmas and grey areas relating to this topic therefore, I think it constitutes as an important modern day issue.

There are many ethical dilemmas within cultural appropriation, for example, when a fashion company exploits a cultural pattern to make income ... Throughout this essay I will be discussing whether or not it is ethically correct for the fashion industry to culturally appropriate symbols or patterns that have been taken from different cultures.

How is this writer building arguments?

Causing Offence

Cultural appropriation has offended a lot of indigenous groups and the public. For example, Victoria's Secret came under fire for appropriating a Native American headdress ... Victoria's Secret presented the headdress on a catwalk show, which was used to promote bikinis ...

However, Britni Danielle commented that ' "cultural appropriation" has become a catchall for those looking to complain about white people who enjoy the food, music, or traditions of other cultures.' This implies that there are people who have become too paranoid about the term 'cultural appropriation.' Therefore, these people are not aware of the differences between cultural appropriation and cultural exchange.

I believe that cultural appropriation could be viewed as a process of celebrating someone else's culture ... However, if an indigenous group's cultural pattern ... has become distorted or manipulated ... then I would believe that it is offensive towards that indigenous community or culture.

How successful is this conclusion?

Conclusion

From this discussion on cultural appropriation and whether it is ethically correct for the fashion industries to use symbols and designs from different cultures, I have concluded that there is no right answer to this issue. Each case has to be looked at in accordance with the relevant criteria and judged on its own merits.

For example, designers have begun promoting different cultures through fashion, which makes a positive impact on our world ... The public have now started to acknowledge different indigenous communities and their patterns, symbols and traditions...

We have become a multi-cultural and inter-connected society through our knowledge and understanding ... Osman Ahmed commented that 'Well-intentioned appropriation can be a force for good, creating a cultural exchange and enriching the vocabulary for designers ...' However, the fashion industry have occasionally been unethical towards these indigenous groups ...

I think it is vital for today's society to have access to a wide variety of cultures ... However, I also believe it is important for the fashion brands or anyone else who borrows a cultural pattern and incorporates them into their project that they attribute the design to that indigenous community ... I also think the fashion industry should produce a code of ethics for the designers [that] prevents them from copying, manipulating or distorting a cultural pattern without of permission.

EXPERT TIP

If you are struggling to structure your ideas, take a break away from your computer – go for a walk before returning to your work.

CHAPTER SUMMARY KEY POINTS

- Criterion C: Critical Thinking is worth up to 12 marks – the most out of any criterion.

- Taking a critical approach to your reflective project is to show analytical and evaluative skills.

- Avoid descriptive writing, as you need to show analytical, evaluative and critical thinking.

- Any source can contain bias or inaccuracies, so it is good practice to challenge the assumptions made about any text you use by asking questions.

- Make sure your own balanced opinion and voice comes through as a result of weighing up information and different perspectives.

In addition to your feedback from your supervisor, use the following questions to reflect on your first draft to inform your RPPF:

Looking at my introduction, do I have a reasoned argument?

Do I maintain this argument throughout my draft?

Have I made clear links between my different points and evidence I have used?

Am I answering my question at the beginning, middle and end of my writing?

Have I been clear in the essay about why I have selected the evidence I have?

Does my conclusion reflect the argument I have established throughout my writing?

Do I offer any solutions and my own thoughts?

Reflective tools I might use:
- Annotate my initial essay plan with reflection on changes that need making
- An annotated draft of my essay using colour-coding and/or comment boxes for REAL and SEAL
- A reflection on this annotation with strengths and weaknesses of my first draft
- Recorded discussion with a peer about a key point I am having difficulties with
- A copy of my bibliography where I have placed the sources in order of relevancy/use/quality

RPPF

Interim reflections – questions to help you evaluate:
- What have you learned from the experience so far and what is the thinking behind your next move?
- Have you had to make any modifications or change your approach?
- What setbacks have you had and how did you turn it around? ('setbacks' might be quality of source material)
- How is this experience matching with your preconceived ideas – is the outcome so far expected or unexpected?

Interim reflections

LEARNER PROFILE ATTRIBUTE

Reflective

The interim reflection is where you are going to evaluate the progress of your reflective project in the RPPF. It is the place where you can respond to the challenges you have faced and the feedback you have had. It is also the place to reflect on the local and global impact emerging in your argument.

Reflect on the challenges you have faced

A closer look at the criteria

The interim reflection is the place to demonstrate just how well you have understood the requirements of the RPPF as it ideally takes place when you are well advanced in the reflective project process; your research is very well developed and you probably will have completed your draft essay already. When you receive and reflect on the feedback from your draft essay, you are in the position to record in the RPPF your reflections on the challenges you have encountered so far and how these can be overcome for the next stage of the project. Or how these challenges were overcome, what was learned from the process and the changes you made as a response. This is what is meant by refining the research process and evaluating the decisions you have made. Remember, this is the place to let your voice come through and show that you are in charge of your learning.

EXAMPLE TASK: ASSESS AN INTERIM REFLECTION

This example of an interim reflection comes from an RPPF that scored 5 out of 6 marks. Using the criteria from the top band below, discuss how the student has reflected. What challenges did they face and what decisions did they make? What attributes of the learner profile did they demonstrate?

During my second reflection with my supervisor I talked about how I was planning to gather new research for my reflective project. For example, I have planned to interview an expert on Cultural Appropriation from WIPO. Therefore, I needed to prepare a series of questions regarding the interview that will be happening next week.

In addition, throughout my research process I have sometimes found myself going in an unexpected journey OR going off in a tangent. For example, I watched a TED video, which was talking about cultural appropriation however, I thought that this video was biased because it did not talk about both sides of the argument (equally). As well the video talked a lot about cultural appropriation within the music industry and not in the fashion industry. However, there were ideas mentioned that could become applicable and useful in my context. I am learning to stay focused and to read between the lines – to analyse what's relevant, taking from the source what is most useful about my topic and to critique the source and work out what aspects of the source could be biased.

As well I have adapted my research question from 'Is it ethically correct to use copied symbols and designs that have been taken from different designers and cultures?' to 'Is it ethically correct for the fashion industry to use symbols and designs that have been taken from different designers and cultures?' Basically I decided to remove the word 'copied' from the question and include the words 'fashion industry' to make sure that the reader knows that this is the focus of the written piece. In addition, I thought it was useful to keep research focused within the fashion industry. My new question limits the scope and takes away the bias.

The top band criteria (5–6 marks)

- There is evidence that student reflection is evaluative.
- Reflections given on decision-making and planning include reference to the student's capacity to consider actions and ideas in response to setbacks experienced in the research process.
- These reflections communicate a high degree of intellectual and personal engagement with the subject and process of research, demonstrating authenticity, intellectual initiative and/or creativity in the student voice.

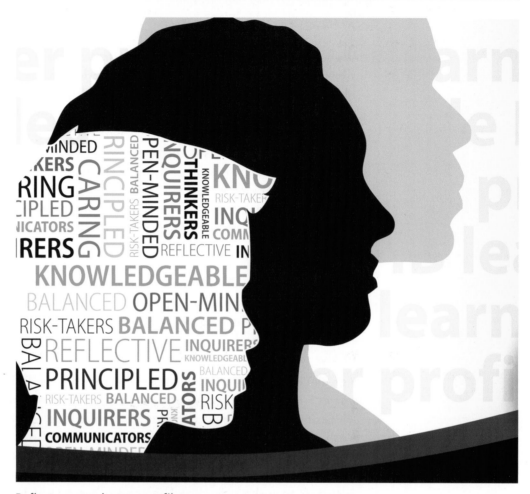

Reflect on your learner profile

ACTIVITY: PRACTISING EMPATHY WITHIN YOUR REFLECTIVE PROJECT AND RPPF

You might be stuck trying to present alternative viewpoints or coming up with your own solutions. Try this reflective tool to help you develop ideas. Remember, you do not have to commit to believing alternative points of view – you are there to identify them and then weigh up the strengths and weaknesses of them.

1 Identify someone in the situation you are examining – maybe someone you are struggling to understand or show sympathy for.

2 Given just the information you have, what might this person be feeling, thinking, knowing or experiencing?

3 Identify what is missing: What might help you understand or sympathise with this person's perspective better?

4 Now what do you notice about your own perspective and how does it feel stepping into someone else's shoes?

This last step would be really interesting to develop in your RPPF.

Inspired by Harvard Project Zero http://www.pz.harvard.edu/search/resources

REFLECTION POINT

What attributes of the learner profile are you finding your greatest strength and your greatest challenge?

CHAPTER SUMMARY KEY POINTS

- Your second reflection for the RPPF is called the interim reflection and takes place after your second official meeting with your supervisor and after you have received your first draft.

- The interim reflection is a time to reflect how far you have progressed since the start of the reflective project.

- The interim reflection is a time to reflect about how far you have left to go.

- The emphasis for this reflection is on analysis and the strengths and weaknesses of the decisions you have made as well as consideration of the challenges you faced.

- Remember that you do not repeat any content from your reflective project in your RPPF.

- Once you have finished your interim reflection, you should not add to it at a later date.

Citation, referencing

WHY DO I CITE AND REFERENCE?

This is to demonstrate you have produced a quality piece of academic research and writing, and ensure you have not plagiarised.

A citation is a short, formal acknowledgement of a source within your work whenever you paraphrase, quote, make use of an idea expressed by somebody else or refer to a specific body of work. What the citation looks like will depend on the referencing system you have used.

A reference is the full bibliographical details of a source.

Referencing is acknowledging the sources of information (books, journals, articles, websites) you have used in your writing both within the body of work as an in-text reference or citation as well as in the list of sources at the end of your work.

A bibliography is list of all sources used in preparing your work, including those that inspired you but which you did not cite in your work.

HOW DO I REFERENCE?

Distinguish between your words and others by the use of quotation marks followed by an appropriate citation that denotes an entry in the bibliography. It does not matter which referencing style you use as long as you do it consistently and do not swap to another system at any stage.

- MLA, APA, Harvard or Chicago are the most common amongst many reference styles.
- Referencing styles usually all include: author, title, date of publication, date of access, publisher, URL for online sources. Online sources also should include the date you accessed them.

and formatting

WHAT DO I CITE/REFERENCE?

- You must give credit to others' work including work that may have inspired you but you have not used directly or works that you may have paraphrased or summarized.
- As well as text sources, you must reference any audio-visual material such as interviews or podcasts, diagrams, images, graphs or any other tables or illustrations.
- Electronic sources must include the date you accessed that information as they can be liable to change. Note down your citations as you write your essay. You have a greater chance of plagiarising unintentionally if you try citing retrospectively.

WHERE CAN I GET HELP?

- Websites such as **www.easybib.com/** or **www.citethisforme.com** are useful tools to help you get started.
- If in doubt, ask for advice from your supervisor or school librarian.
- In the IB's Programme Resource Centre there is a document called *Effective citing and referencing.*

WHAT IS THE WORD COUNT AND WHAT IS INCLUDED IN THIS?

Option 1 of the reflective project has a word limit of 3,000 words. You must assume the examiner will stop reading after 3,000 words.

Option 2 includes a written essay of 1,500–2,000 words accompanied by an additional format such as a film, oral presentation, interview, play or display (be clear on the different lengths required for each one).

- The word count does NOT include:
  - acknowledgements
  - the contents page
  - maps, charts, diagrams, annotated illustrations and tables
  - equations, formulas and calculations
  - citations or references
  - footnotes or endnotes
  - the bibliography
  - appendices.
- Do not use appendices to address assessment criteria as the examiner might not read them; your project should be complete in itself. You can include photos, cartoons, graphs, charts and so on but make sure they are relevant and acknowledged correctly.
- The RPPF is separate from the main body of work and has a limit of 1,000 words.

The final draft

LEARNER PROFILE ATTRIBUTES		
Principled	Thinker	Communicator

Academic honesty in the final stages

You are nearly there. These last stages of the reflective project are about paying close attention to the small details before taking a step back and reflecting on the whole process.

REFLECTION POINT

Consider how you have demonstrated each of the characteristics of the learner profile during the entire reflective project journey; the integrity and respect you have shown here has led you to an academically honest piece of work you should be proud of.

As you have learned throughout this process, academic honesty is the backbone of the reflective project; it has to be your own work based on your individual, original ideas whilst explicitly acknowledging others' work and ideas. It is worthwhile remembering that plagiarism, by definition, is using the work of others without acknowledging you have done so – intentionally or unintentionally.

EXPERT TIP

Make sure you have followed this process consistently throughout your project: you have distinguished between your words and others' using quotation marks followed by an appropriate citation that denotes an entry in the bibliography.

■ A look at the criteria

Criterion D can be easily overlooked, as it does not appear to be worth many marks. It might be a relief to you that there is not too much emphasis on communication style but this is deceptive as excellent communication skills are implicit in achieving highly in all the other criteria. Looking at this criterion more closely really helps in the final stages of the reflective project as it makes you pay attention to the accuracy of structure and content. Pay particular close attention if you have chosen Option 2 and that your two pieces have cohesive structures that complement each other.

Criterion D: Communication. This criterion assesses the way in which the student presents a structured and coherent project through their communication style, using appropriate terminology accurately and consistently, assisting to convey ideas and concepts clearly.

Markband descriptor

0	The work does not reach the standard of the descriptor below	
1	There is a straightforward structure to the project as a whole, with similar material grouped together in a logical manner	
2	Communication is generally clear and structured appropriately, with consistent use of appropriate terminology	
3	Communication is coherent and structured in a way that supports the understanding of the student's ideas and arguments, with effective use of appropriate terminology to support and develop ideas	

■ Citations and references for academic honesty

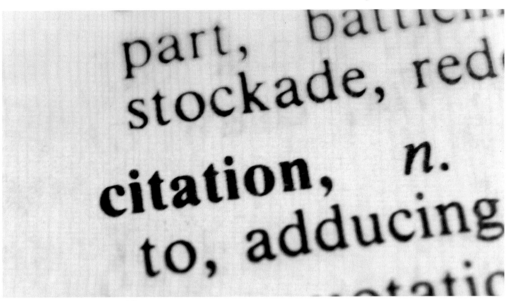

Make your sources visible

To score highly in Criterion A, you need to show 'there is evidence of excellent planning of research, and the determination and collection of appropriate and varied sources'. This means you need to acknowledge all sources clearly.

What is a citation? A citation is a short, formal acknowledgement of a source within your work whenever you paraphrase, quote, make use of an idea expressed by somebody else or refer to a specific body of work. What the citation looks like will depend on the referencing system you have used but can be in-text citations, footnotes or end-notes clearly placed next to the quotation or paraphrased text you have written, as well as the author's last name and page number if there is one.

EXAMPLE TASK: CITATIONS

Look at this example of the different ways citing can be embedded into your writing and how in each case its purpose is to acknowledge the ideas of another text whilst reinforcing the writer's own ideas.

… It may be human nature to think that we are more astute than we really are, to see what we want to see and to ignore that which might work against us. It could be that, "More often than not, risk takers underestimate the odds they face, and do not invest sufficient effort to find out what the odds are." (Kahneman, 2011, p. 256).

… As Kahneman puts it, "More often than not, risk takers underestimate the odds they face, and do not invest sufficient effort to find out what the odds are" (2011, p. 256).

… Kahneman's research (2011) suggests that "More often than not, risk takers underestimate the odds they face, and do not invest sufficient effort to find out what the odds are" (p. 256).

… In 2011, behavioural economist Daniel Kahneman suggested "More often than not, risk takers underestimate the odds they face, and do not invest sufficient effort to find out what the odds are" (p. 256).

… Daniel Kahneman, awarded the Nobel Prize for Economics in 2002, has shown that "More often than not, risk takers underestimate the odds they face, and do not invest sufficient effort to find out what the odds are" (2011, p. 256).

Source: Royce, John. 'Citation and Referencing.' *IB Review*, vol.2, no.4, Hodder Education, April 2016, pp. 13–15.

Lastly, all citations should be fully referenced in the bibliography.

Websites such as **www.citethisforme.com** will provide you with the correct formatting for your citation and your bibliography within a referencing system of your choice.

■ What is referencing?

Be consistent in your referencing style

A reference is simply the full bibliographical details of a source you have used. The act of referencing is acknowledging the sources of information (books, journals, articles, websites) you have used in your writing both within the body of work as an in-text reference or citation as well as in the list of sources at the end of your work. It is worth remembering that a bibliography is a list of all sources used in preparing your work, including those that inspired you but which you might not have cited in your work.

■ Choosing an appropriate referencing style

The IB does not prescribe which referencing system you should use but whatever reference style you do choose, use it consistently throughout your entire project and do not swap to another system at any stage. The minimum information you must include in a reference is: name of author, date of publication, title of source and page numbers if applicable. You have been encouraged throughout this process to research all sorts of texts so it is likely that you will have a varied bibliography; it is important to remember that the citations and referencing will likely differ in detail and format within a referencing system.

Below are some examples from the Harvard referencing style that you might have already seen in the research you have done. It is worth investigating other referencing styles such as MHRA, which specifically uses footnotes instead of in-text citations, which you might prefer.

Harvard – full references for bibliography

Book: Last name, First initial. (Year published). *Title*. Edition. (Only include the edition if it is not the first edition.) City published: Publisher, Page(s).

Online Journal: Last name, First initial. (Year published). Article Title. *Journal*, [online] Volume(Issue), pages. Available at: URL [Accessed Day Mo. Year].

Print journal: Last name, First initial. (Year published). Article title. *Journal*, Volume (Issue), Page(s).

Website: Last name, First initial. (Year published). Page title. [online] Website name. Available at: URL [Accessed Day Mo. Year].

If no author details are available, include the website name and the year published instead.

Artwork: Last name, First initial. (Year created). Title. [Medium]. City that the artwork is/ was displayed in: Gallery or Museum.

Blogs: Last name, First initial. (Year published). Post title. [Blog] Blog name. Available at: URL [Accessed Day Mo. Year].

Broadcasts: *Series title*, (Year published). [Type of Programme] Channel number: Broadcaster

DVD, Video or Film: *Film title*. (Year published). [Format] Place of origin: Film maker.

Government publications: Government Agency OR Last name, First Initial. (Year published). *Title of Document or Article*. City published: Publisher, Page(s).

Online images or videos: Last name, First initial. OR Corporate Author. (Year published). *Title/description*. [format] Available at: URL [Accessed Day Mo. Year].

Harvard – in-text citations

Students use in-text citations to indicate the specific parts of their paper that were paraphrased or quoted directly from a source. Each in-text citation generally displays the last name of the author and the year the source was published. The in-text citation is usually located at the end of the quoted or paraphrased sentence (Source: **www. citethisforme.com**).

If the author has already been referred to in the sentence then all that is needed is the date of publication in parentheses (brackets) after the quotation.

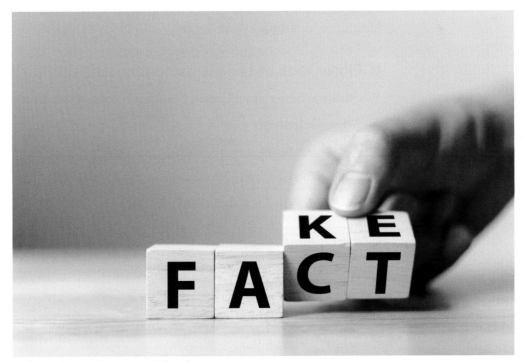

Referencing online materials takes care

■ Using and referencing online materials

In Chapter 6, we discussed the pitfalls of internet research. It would be highly unusual given the nature of the reflective project for your bibliography not to have online materials. Within whatever referencing system you are using, make sure that you have as a minimum the following information:

■ The title of the online material used

■ The full website address

■ The author (if possible)

■ The date it was accessed

This last point is important, especially when writing about current, global ethical concerns where information, research and perspectives can change quickly; if you include the date you accessed and used this online information, it can be checked that at the time of your research and writing, these details were correct.

EXAMPLE TASK: BIBLIOGRAPHY

Discuss this excerpt from a reflective project bibliography. Look at format, content and structure. What sort of sources have they used?

Bollier, David, and Laurie Racine. "Ready to Share: Creativity in Fashion & Digital Culture." *Learcentre*, Ready to Share: Fashion the Ownership of Creativity, 25. Jan. 2005, learcenter.org/pdf/RTSBollierRacine.pdf

Carson, Shelley. "Plagiarism and Its Effect on Creative Work." *Psychology Today*, Sussex Publishers, 16 Oct, 2010, www.psychologytoday.com/blog/life-art/201010/plagiarism-and-its-effect-creative-work

"Crimes of Fashion: Intellectual Property and Indigenous Dress." *Global Notes*, 13, Apr. 2016. publish.illinois.edu/iaslibrary/tag/indigenous

Danielle, Britni. "Have We Gotten Too Paranoid About Cultural Appropriation?" Clutch Magazine, clutchmagazineonline.com/2014/05/gotten-paranoid-cultural-apprpriation/

■ Closer look at the assessment criteria and different formats

Whether you have chosen Option 1 or 2, you need to consider how you include:

■ Acknowledgements

■ The contents page

■ Maps, charts, diagrams, annotated illustrations and tables

■ Equations, formulas and calculations

■ Citations or references (whether parenthetical or numbered)

■ Footnotes or endnotes

■ The bibliography

■ Appendices.

EXAMPLE TASK: CONTENTS PAGE

Look at the following contents page of a reflective project. Has everything been included? What are the strengths and weaknesses of this contents page?

Is it ethically correct for the fashion industry to use the symbols and designs of different cultures?

ACTIVITY: ACTING ON FEEDBACK

You will have had feedback from your supervisor and they may have used open questions and comments like the ones below (also suggested in Chapter 7). Make sure you carry out the list of checks suggested here in addition to your supervisor's feedback.

Possible open questions and comments:

- Do you notice anything here?
- Could you make this clearer?
- What are you missing here?
- Could this belong elsewhere?
- Have you a voice?
- Check for consistency here.
- Check the accuracy here.
- Check you are meeting requirements here for citations/bibliographies/appendices.

- Check you have answered all your questions and included all your relevant research.

These open questions could prompt you to check:

- if your question has stayed the same throughout
- if you have understood the full ethical impact of a perspective or idea
- if you have constructed your analysis using REAL and SEAL (see Chapter 8)
- if you have included useful information in an appendix that belongs in the main work
- if your argument is unbalanced
- if your conclusion does not take into account all the arguments you have put forward
- if you have included your own ideas and offered possible solutions to your dilemma.

ACTIVITY: MARK YOUR REFLECTIVE PROJECT

Further activities to help your understanding of assessment criteria for the final draft.

There is no better way to check your final draft before submission than to mark it yourself in the way your supervisor will. Your supervisor will write on your final draft where you are meeting each criteria and whether it is developing throughout your work.

Suggestion 1: You can take each criterion in turn or, if you are feeling more confident, apply each criterion as they come up.

Suggestion 2: Some students find it easier to go back to a colour-coding system for Criteria A–D and then you can see how well you are applying the criteria. An absence of one colour consistently throughout your essay might denote that it is not fully developed.

Suggestion 3: Go through your work and see if you can apply the following words to your work. This exercise can be easier if working with a partner and discussing each other's work but you must make sure they have a completely different topic and career-related subject to you!

Colour-coding is a good checking system

A Excellent, effective, well-focused, analytical, critical, sustained, accurate, documented, reflective, forward-thinking, conceptual, personal, academically honest

B Good, consistent, appropriate, analytical, critical, reasoned, relevant, accurate, reflective, documented, clear, academically honest

C Partially effective, mostly appropriate, mostly accurate, sometimes analytical, factual, informative, descriptive, partially reflective, satisfactory, academically honest

REFLECTION POINT

You have focused on specific criterion throughout this book as you have developed skills. Now look over all the criteria in the mark scheme and consider where your work stands. However, do remember that if you have fully embraced every step of the reflective project process, you have achieved far more than a mark.

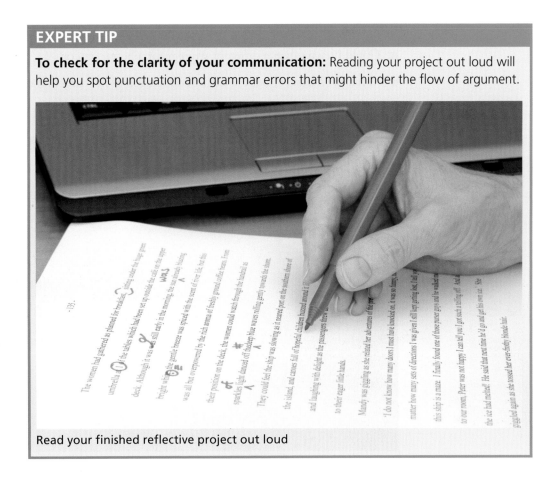

EXPERT TIP

To check for the clarity of your communication: Reading your project out loud will help you spot punctuation and grammar errors that might hinder the flow of argument.

Read your finished reflective project out loud

◼ Final checks and the final section of the RPPF

Before you submit your final copy and RPPF to your supervisor by the deadline your school sets, you will want to check everything is in order. After all, your reflective project needs to achieve the minimum of a D grade if you are to obtain the full IBCP certificate. Reading your work again before submission as well as before writing your last reflection in your RPPF helps to:

- check for the small details that are crucial such as acknowledging all sources you have used and ensuring the format is correct

- evaluate the strength of your argument, your personal voice and conclusions you offer

- take a step back and consider how far you have come in the process and how your personal opinions, knowledge and methodology may have changed.

Once you have finished your final draft, it is time to take a step back and reflect on how far you have come by looking over your RRS, your final draft, as well as your initial and interim reflections in your RPPF. Your final reflection is not about whether you have produced a perfect piece of work; it is about the process and your interaction with the ethical dilemma you chose as its focus. You might discuss the following type of questions with your supervisor before writing your final reflection.

- Do I feel I have fulfilled the expectations of the reflective project?

- Where do I stand now in relation to the ethical dilemma in the question?

- How have my views been challenged or changed by the work I have done?

- What were the most effective research strategies I learned to use?

- Which skills will be most useful in the future?
- Could I have taken a different strategy for a better outcome?
- What did I learn about the ethical dimension of my career-related subject?

How far have you come?

CHAPTER SUMMARY KEY POINTS

- Referencing is used to acknowledge and credit the work of others cited in your reflective project.

- Use citation and referencing when referring to the work, words or thoughts of others.

- Citation within a text shows just how academically honest you are being and your referencing is an integral part of academic honesty.

- Good citation and references demonstrate the depth of your research and critical skills.

- The inclusion of references adds strength to your arguments and allow you to demonstrate your analytical skills.

- Record your sources throughout the research process and essay writing rather than at the end.

- Read your final reflective project carefully for punctuation and grammar errors that might hinder the flow of argument.

- For your final reflection, take a step back and reflect on how far you have come by looking over your RRS, your final draft as well as your initial and interim reflections in your RPPF.

Managing the Reflective Project process

Understand the requirements

Assessment criteria
Research question
Formal presentation (word limit, citations and referencing)
Uploaded RPPF

Get started

The reflective project process is 50 hours
Make a plan and tackle the process in bite-size chunks
Do not panic if you get behind: review, adapt and get back to it

Managing the reflective project process

Keep it manageable and engaging

Use the SMARTER Code to help you:
Specific – What exactly will you do?
Measurable – How will you know you've succeeded?
Achievable – Is it realistic?
Resourced – Have you allocated enough time? Have you enough information?
Timetabled – By when will you achieve each step?
Evaluated – Keep checking you are on track
Reflective – Sometimes, changed circumstances mean a modification in the goal is necessary

Give yourself rewards along the way for meeting deadlines and achieving difficult tasks

Time and process management

LEARNER PROFILE ATTRIBUTES		
Communicator	Reflective	Caring

Overall, the reflective project will take 50 hours to complete over the course of a year. This may seem a lot but when you consider each step of the process, you realize it reflects the amount of time needed to truly get the most out of the reflective project journey.

It is important to be organized from the start and break down the whole process into manageable chunks. Your teachers will probably give you a suggested timeline with key assessment opportunities throughout the year; they will do this to help you keep on track and stop you from becoming overwhelmed or leaving it too late. However, it is a good idea to create your own timeline that includes not just the school's requirements for the reflective project but also other assessments and pressure points from your other subjects too.

A general timeline might include: Key stages and date to be achieved

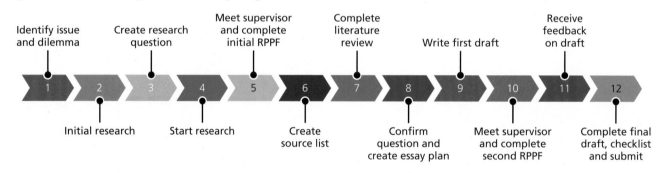

A detailed timeline that takes into account detailed stages of the process might look like this: Key stages and date to be achieved

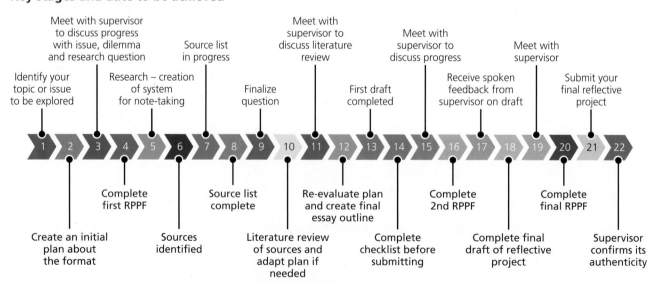

A well-constructed timeline keeps the process manageable

▨ Creating your bespoke timeline

Use the SMARTER Code to help you:

Specific – What exactly will you do?

Measurable – How will you know you've succeeded?

Achievable – Is it realistic?

Resourced – Have you allocated enough time? Have you enough information?

Timetabled – By when will you achieve each step?

Evaluated – Keep checking you are on track

Reflective –Sometimes changed circumstances mean a modification in the goal is necessary.

Give yourself rewards along the way for meeting deadlines and achieving difficult tasks.

▨ Work habits

Many students claim they work best when sitting with friends with a laptop open, which many teachers doubt. Even if this is how you produce your best work, you should be honest right from the start about creating an approach that will allow you to engage in the process and help you avoid procrastination.

How do you work best?

REFLECTION POINT

Consider:
- Do you work best with music or buzz around you?
- Do you need complete silence?
- Do you know how your friends work best and are you respectful of this?
- Do you work best at school or at home?
- Do you work best at a certain time of day?
- When are you able to devote time to this?
- How will you access resources?
- Where will you keep your RRS?

What environment do you need to create to be the Learner profile?

Monitoring progress

Your teacher in charge of the reflective project will probably have a shared online document with you and your supervisor to monitor you achieving certain milestones and sticking to deadlines. It is important you are proactive here and do not get into the habit of being chased. This is your project and your attitude needs to reflect exactly how you would behave in the workplace if you were given an independent project to carry out. Be aware of the needs of others in your community throughout this process too.

Possible pitfalls and troubleshooting

Every step of the reflective project is both an opportunity and a challenge. Some areas might not go well, you get stuck or life outside of the project demands your attention. The IBCP is a challenging course and the reflective project is just one element of it, so it is not a failure if you struggle with any part of this process or get behind. The one thing you must try to do is communicate and talk to your supervisor or another member of staff who can help.

Mindfulness for the stressed student

What do you do to keep calm?

REFLECTION POINT

At moments of stress or just feeling overwhelmed, it's good to have ways of taking yourself out of the situation you are dealing with. It's good to have a place you can go to that you know calms you and you can have a moment to relax. Students have found the following ideas helpful to get back on track when their studies become a little too much. It's important you find a way to have time out and look after yourself.

- Exercise whether running, walking, hula hooping, martial arts
- Read something unconnected to your studies
- Breathe deeply
- Yoga or meditation
- Mindfulness apps
- Engaging in the community and helping others
- Review your routine
- Create a bucket list of things you want to achieve
- Get outside in nature
- Go to an art gallery
- Watch a film or documentary
- Play a childhood game
- Draw

Make sure you have time out

CHAPTER SUMMARY KEY POINTS

- A well-constructed and clear timeline is essential to keep you on track.

- Breakdown your reflective project process into manageable chunks.

- Share your timeline with your supervisor.

- Work SMARTER.

- Be honest about your working habits and do not panic if you get behind.

- Keep communicating throughout the process with your supervisor and teachers.

- Do not underestimate the final stages of the project and the checks you will make.

- Give yourself rewards for meeting milestones.

Final submission checklist

Your reflective project does not have to have a prescribed structure but must have the following features:

An ethical issue ☐

The ethical dilemma ☐

Research question ☐

Research ☐

Critical analysis of the ethical dilemma ☐

Citations, references and bibliography ☐

Areas to check closely:

Cover page ☐

Declaration of authenticity ☐

Research question ☐

Contents page ☐

Research methods ☐

Ethical perspectives ☐

Analysis, discussion and critical thinking ☐

Conclusion ☐

Reflections ☐

Format and formal presentation ☐

Bibliography ☐

12 Final submission

Final submission

What happens to your reflective project once you have submitted your final draft?

The reflective project and RPPF is internally marked and externally moderated. What this means is that your school will mark all their reflective projects fully and submit all the marks to the IB. The IB system will generate a request for a random sample of these reflective projects depending on the size of the cohort, and your school will submit these with each accompanying RPPF electronically. An external moderator will then read these projects closely and check that they agree with the marks your school has given. They will either agree with the marks that have been given or make a few adjustments if they feel the marks that have been rewarded are a little low or high. This will be your final mark.

Monday	Tuesday	Wednesday	Thursday	Friday	Satur
29	30	31	~~1~~	~~2~~	~~3~~
~~5~~	~~6~~	~~7~~	~~8~~	~~9~~	~~10~~
~~12~~	~~13~~	(14)	15	16	17

Will you be ready?

■ Submission requirements: Uploading of RPPF and marked reflective project

■ Marking the final draft

Your supervisor will mark your final draft by applying the criteria that you have been working with throughout this process. If you have been meeting with your supervisor regularly, you will appreciate that they are the person who knows best the process you have personally been through to complete this element. Like your first draft, they will not mark for spelling and grammar or correct anything. Marking the reflective project is more of an interactive process where your supervisor might write several times on each page in the margins and/or give comments in an overview on how you are achieving particular criteria. This is a process that helps them come to a decision about your final mark, as well as show the external reflective project moderator why they have come to their marks. They also will probably write concluding remarks related to each of the criteria at the end of your project as well as fill in the allocated supervisor comment box on your RPPF.

■ What does high-achieving work look like for each criteria?

You may wonder how your supervisor makes decisions about the mark for each criterion. In the IB Reflective Project Guide, guidance is given for what work will look like within the different bands of that criterion. Supervisors are advised to take a best-fit approach. Below is the top of Criteria A–E.

ACTIVITY: WHERE DOES YOUR WORK STAND?

Using these markers, how would you judge your work? Using the marking criteria in Chapter 1, what mark would you give yourself for each criterion?

Criterion A: Focus and method

■ Work in this band includes a question that provides the opportunity to evaluate the implications of the ethical dilemma beyond simply giving the case for and against. For example, 'Should terminally ill individuals have the option of physician-assisted suicide?' allows the student to explore a wider range of perspectives at a theoretical (medical, legal, moral) and personal (doctor, patient, family) level.

■ Source materials are well chosen, varied and are often used with precision to illustrate particular points, arguments and ideas. Work in this band is likely to take account of aspects such as value judgments, bias and misrepresentation of evidence/statistics in their responses and comment on them where appropriate.

Criterion B: Knowledge and understanding in context

■ Work in this band is beginning to be more nuanced (e.g. becoming aware of the subtleties, ironies and contradictions within the different perspectives: The hazard to wildlife/visual impact on the landscape of the most 'green' source of power), although this may not be sustained throughout the whole response.

■ A range of different perspectives/viewpoints is analysed and evaluated rather than just presented/contrasted. There is justification of the validity and weaknesses of different arguments and balance between them when drawing conclusions (e.g. large upfront investment required to build wind turbines balanced against low running costs).

■ Similarly, the impact on communities and/or global and cultural perspectives is considered and, where appropriate, balanced (e.g. impact on rural communities of wind turbines, the economic impact on mining communities of decreasing reliance on coal balanced with the global environmental benefits of clean renewable energy).

Criterion C: Critical thinking

■ In this band, points made and evidence chosen combine to develop a clear and coherent argument, moving with confidence between taking an overview of the subject and engaging with specific details and evidence.

■ Understanding of concepts such as cause and effect is becoming more developed and nuanced, for example by considering different unintended negative consequences of positive actions (Diverting resources into cancer treatments leads to lower funding for social care and a reduction in the quality of life for a larger number of patients with less serious, chronic conditions).

■ Conclusions tend to draw on, but not simply repeat, ideas, evidence and arguments from earlier in the response, providing an effective overview of the issue and the associated ethical dilemma.

■ Work in this band begins to synthesize, rather than simply select and present, evidence, bringing together ideas and information from different sources to support and develop the argument.

Criterion D: Communication

■ The structure of the report is organized to develop an overall argument. Each section builds effectively on what has gone before, leading to a logical conclusion.

■ Terminology is used clearly and precisely to support and develop ideas.

Criterion E: Engagement and reflection

■ Work in this band expresses and explains how the student's understanding of the issue and related ethical dilemma has changed and developed and what new insights they have gained as a result of undertaking the project.

■ Work in this band justifies the approach taken to developing a research method, often linking it explicitly to the chosen issue and related ethical dilemma (e.g. showing understanding that different forms of evidence can have different effects – a graph could show the scale of an issue precisely, but a first-person account may have a more emotional impact).

■ There is evidence in the work that the student is beginning to develop their own ideas and insights rather than re-presenting the views of others. Evidence of initiative in research methods could include effective primary research (e.g. seeking an interview with someone directly involved in or affected by the issue).

In 2018 the following grade boundaries were set at:

Mark range/36	Grades A–E
28–36	A
23–27	B
17–22	C
11–16	D
0–10	E

A pass of 11 out of 36 was the minimum that could be achieved to pass with a D grade and achieve the full IBCP.

How do you rate your final essay?

CHAPTER SUMMARY KEY POINTS

- Check your reflective project has a structure with an ethical issue, the ethical dilemma, research question, research, critical analysis of the ethical dilemma, citations, references and bibliography.

- You need a D grade in the reflective project to achieve the full IBCP certificate.

- Your supervisor will mark your final draft.

- Your supervisor will mark it like your first draft, looking for criteria met.

- Your supervisor will authenticate your work; they will officially confirm that it is academically honest.

Appendix

Tips for a successful Reflective Project

1 Consider both Option 1 and 2 in detail before making a decision.

2 Take time to understand the reflective project objectives at the start of the process but return to them throughout the process.

3 Try different reflective strategies right from the start in the RRS.

4 Always choose a topic you find interesting and will keep you interested.

5 Practice looking for multiple perspectives and not just two sides to an ethical issue.

6 Take time with your question and don't be afraid to review and revise it.

7 Carry out research in an academically honest way by recording your research in a responsible way.

8 Manage your time by creating a timeline with key stages you know you might find tricky.

9 Use the criteria to help you improve your draft and not just your supervisor's feedback.

10 Work hard on developing your own ideas and bringing out your own voice in your reflective project.

Top tips for successful supervision

1 Try to find a regular time you are able to meet your supervisor.

2 Keep an online log and update it straight after your meeting.

3 At the end of each meeting, arrange your next meeting.

4 Access exemplar material early on to discuss with your supervisor.

5 Make sure you go with your RRS to meetings as well as key questions.

6 If the supervision process breaks down at all, make sure you communicate with a teacher that can help as soon as possible.

7 Be proactive and prepared to start supervisory sessions with a detailed update of your progress.

8 Be honest and upfront if you are behind – don't hide or procrastinate.

9 Make sure you have enough time to receive feedback properly on your draft.

10 Never expect the supervisor to be an expert; they are there to observe, discuss, encourage and ask helpful questions so the student can take ownership of their whole reflective project experience.

Top tips for reflection and evaluation

1 Recognize that the entire project is about reflection; reflection on your own journey through a dilemma but also reflection on multiple other perspectives that emerge from your research question.

2 Reflection can be diverse and not just writing at length and asking the same questions; having a researcher's reflection space (RRS), whether a physical book or online journal, will allow you to record ideas and questions in a spontaneous, natural way – often ideas come to us when we least expect it.

3 Be prepared to reflect on the successes and setbacks of your chosen dilemma, question, research methods, other people's arguments and possible solutions.

4 Failures and setbacks are not a hindrance to reflection; if you can understand what has happened and why it has not worked, this is a valuable part of the process and mirrors what will happen in the world of work.

5 Set aside time to write each of your three key reflections at the start, after your feedback and once you have finished your final draft; once they are complete, do not go back to them.

6 If you write all your reflections at the end, be philosophical about not achieving a high mark in Criterion E.

7 The word 'evaluate' can be vague and overused. Have strategies to help you deeply analyse the data, ideas and viewpoints that you come across.

8 Remember not just to analyse *what* is said, but *where* that idea came from, *why* it was said and *how* reliable it is.

9 Keep yourself at the centre of this process – you may be considering different examples, perspectives and cultures but how you take all these into account and come up with your own ideas, predictions and solutions is crucial.

10 Make sure you find a focus that you can feel passionate about so you can say confidently why it is important to you, your community and the wider world.

Reflective Project checklist

Cover page (Title page)

Have you included the research question?	☐
Have you stated your personal code?	☐
Have you included the word count?	☐

Declaration of authenticity

Have you included a signed declaration of authenticity?	☐
Have you dated the declaration of authenticity?	☐
Have you submitted the declaration of authenticity to your supervisor?	☐

Research question

Is your RQ clearly stated?	☐
Is your RQ consistent throughout the project and does not change?	☐
Is the ethical issue in your RQ clear?	☐
Is the ethical dilemma in your RQ clear?	☐
Is there no bias implicit in your RQ?	☐
Is the topic area clearly relevant to the career-related subject?	☐

Contents page

Have you included a contents page?	☐
Have you used section headings?	☐
Does this include page numbers?	☐
Have you checked the page numbers are accurate?	☐

Research methods

Have you used a sufficient range of appropriate sources?	☐
Is there evidence of sources selected and assessed carefully?	☐
Have you provided evidence of considering the implications of different sources?	☐
Have you established the parameters of your discussion in your introduction?	☐

Analysis, discussion and critical thinking

Have you made it clear in your introduction why your issue and dilemma is relevant to your CRS?	☐
Have you used subject-specific terminology appropriately and consistently?	☐
Have you explained the significance of the data and information you have collected?	☐
Are your points supported by evidence?	☐
Are your arguments consistent with the examples you are providing?	☐
Have you assessed the strengths and weaknesses of different viewpoints?	☐
Have you assessed the strengths and weaknesses of different sources?	☐
Have you provided your own evaluations of sources and perspectives?	☐

Conclusion

Do you clearly come back to the question in your conclusion?	☐
Does your conclusion draw together the arguments you have discussed?	☐
Do you provide possible solutions to your issue and dilemma?	☐
Do you provide further questions that have come from your analysis?	☐

Reflections

Have you completed all three reflection sessions?	☐
Have you demonstrated engagement with your research question and research process?	☐
Do you provide evidence of your thought processes and decision making?	☐
Have you considered challenges you faced or changes of direction?	☐

Format and formal presentation

If you chose Option 1, is your essay 3,000 words?	☐
If you chose Option 2, do your two components comply with word count and length?	☐
Have you used a readable font such as Arial or Times New Roman?	☐
Is your work in font size 12?	☐
Are all your pages numbered?	☐
Are graphs/charts/images/illustrations numbered?	☐
Are graphs/charts/images/illustrations captioned?	☐
Are graphs/charts/images/illustrations referenced appropriately?	☐
Do your page numbers in table of contents match up with the pages?	☐
Have you proofread all your work for spelling, punctuation and grammar errors?	☐
Have you used a consistent system to cite and reference your sources?	☐
Have you used quotation marks properly and consistently?	☐
Have you cited the source of every quotation?	☐
Have you checked you have attributed every quotation explicitly?	☐
Have you clearly shown where you have used the ideas of others?	☐
Does the appendix (if used) contain only relevant and necessary information?	☐
Does the appendix (if used) have a title and an appropriate source?	☐
Are each of the appendix items (if used) clearly mentioned in the text of the essay?	☐
Are all references to items in the appendix clearly cross-referenced, including the relevant page numbers?	☐

Bibliography (Works cited or References)

Have you included a bibliography, containing all your sources used to research and write the reflective project?	■
Has the bibliography been produced in alphabetical order?	■
Do your citations in the body of the essay match the correct references in the bibliography?	■
Does your bibliography list every source used in your reflective project?	■
Does your bibliography use a referencing system consistently?	■
Does your bibliography specify at least author(s), title, date of publication and the publisher for every reference?	■
Is your punctuation consistent?	■

Others

Have you submitted a hard copy of your RP to your supervisor?	■
Are you ready to submit your reflective project?	■

References

Addis, T. (2019), Ethics vs Morals – Difference and Comparison, Diffen. [online] Available at: www.diffen.com/difference/Ethics_vs_Morals [Accessed 1 January 2019].

Additional Guidance for the Reflective Project (2015), Geneva: IB Publishing Ltd.

Amnesty.org. (2019), What We Do. [online] Available at: www.amnesty.org/en/what-we-do/ [Accessed 1 January 2019].

Aristotle and Ross, W. (1908), *The Nicomachean Ethics of Aristotle*. Oxford: Clarendon Press.

Brink-Budgen, R. and Thwaites, J. (2012), *OCR AS Critical Thinking*. Deddington: Philip Allan Updates.

Cite This For Me (2019), Save Time and Improve your Marks with CiteThisForMe, The No. 1 Citation Tool. [online] Available at: www.citethisforme.com/ [Accessed 1 November 2018].

Connolly, L. (2015), Joseph Fletcher's 'Situation Ethics'. [video] Available at: https://youtu.be/WgjldswNP14 [Accessed 1 January 2019].

Crash Course (2016), Aristotle & Virtue Theory: Crash Course Philosophy #38. [video] Available at: https://youtu.be/PrvtOWEXDIQ [Accessed 1 January 2019].

Crash Course (2016), Kant & Categorical Imperatives: Crash Course Philosophy #35. [video] Available at: https://youtu.be/8bIys6JoEDw [Accessed 1 January 2019].

Dimmock, M. and Fisher, A. (2019), Chapter 3. Aristotelian Virtue Ethics. Books.openedition. org. [online] Available at: https://books.openedition.org/obp/4421?lang=en#tocfrom1n1 [Accessed 1 January 2019].

John, R. (2016), 'Citation and Referencing', *IB Review*, 2(4), 13–15.

New Scientist (2017), The Ethics Issue: The 10 biggest moral dilemmas in science. [online] Available at: www.newscientist.com/round-up/ethics-issue [Accessed 1 November 2018].

Professional and Personal Skills Guide (for first use 2016) (2015), Geneva: IB Publishing Ltd.

Pz.harvard.edu. (2019). Homepage Project Zero. [online] Available at: www.pz.harvard.edu/ [Accessed 8 May 2019].

Reflective Project Guide: For use from August 2016 (2016), Geneva: IB Publishing Ltd.

Reflective Project Student Guide (for first use 2016) 2015, Geneva: IB Publishing.

Singer, P. (1994), *Ethics*. Oxford, New York: Oxford University Press.

Singer, P. (2011), *Practical Ethics*. Cambridge: Cambridge University Press.

Syracuse University School of Education (2018), Common Ethical Issues | Syracuse University School of Education. [online] Available at: https://soe.syr.edu/departments/academic/counseling-human-services/modules/ethical/ [Accessed 1 January 2019].

Vardy, P. and Grosch, P. (1994), *The Puzzle of Ethics*. London: Harper Collins Publishers.

Will, B. (2018), Strengths and Weaknesses of Virtue Ethics. [online] Available at: www.bloodyalevels.com/strengths-and-weaknesses-of-virtue-ethics/ [Accessed 1 January 2019].

William David, R. (n.d.), Nicomachean Ethics of Aristotle Index. [online] Available at: http://sacred-texts.com/cla/ari/nico/index.htm [Accessed 1 January 2019].

www.bbc.co.uk. (2014), BBC – Ethics - Introduction to Ethics: Situation ethics. [online] Available at: www.bbc.co.uk/ethics/introduction/situation_1.shtml [Accessed 1 January 2019].

www.bbc.com. (2019), A Question of Ethics. [online] Available at: www.bbc.com/ideas/playlists/a-question-of-ethics [Accessed 1 January 2019].

Yeliz Gülcan, N. (2015), *Discussing the Importance of Teaching Ethics in Education*. [ebook] Adapazari, Sakarya University: Elsevier Ltd, p.2622. Available at: www.sciencedirect.com [Accessed 1 Dec. 2018].

youtube (2016), The Power of the Powerless [Václav Havel]. [video] Available at: https://youtu.be/oSMwrJ-KMxU [Accessed 1 January 2019].

Index

Acknowledgements

The author would personally like to thank Chris and Martha for their love and patience, as well as her marvellous parents and sisters for all their support. Thank you also to the wide circle of friends and colleagues for their reflective wisdom – in particular, George and Martina for their endless encouragement. And to Frank who continues to be an inspiration. Particular acknowledgement and thanks must go to Alanna Fraser for her help with critical and ethical thinking and Alexandra Juniper and Zena Lawton for their kind assistance with exemplars.

The Publishers would like to thank the following for permission to reproduce copyright material.

Every effort has been made to trace all copyright holders, but if any have been inadvertently overlooked, the Publishers will be pleased to make the necessary arrangements at the first opportunity.

Photo credits:

t = top *m* = middle *b* = bottom *r* = right *l* = left

pp.2–3, 12–13, 22–23, 34–35, 48–49, 54–55, 68–69, 76–77, 86–87, 92–93, 103, 108 © ray8/stock.adobe.com; **p.4** © Likee68/stock.adobe.com; **p.14** © Scottiebumich/stock.adobe.com; **p. 30** *t* © Chris Titze Imaging/stock.adobe.com; *b* © Bettmann/Getty Images; **p.31** © Sdecoret/stock.adobe.com; **p.36** © Flavijus Piliponis/stock.adobe.com; **p.37** © ~Bitter~/stock.adobe.com; **p.38** © Argus – Fotolia; **p.40** *t* © Pathdoc/stock.adobe.com; *b* © nickolae – Fotolia; **p.42** © Georgios Kollidas/stock.adobe.com; **p.44** © Dragomirescu/stock.adobe.com; **p.46** © Scherl/Süddeutsche Zeitung Photo/Alamy stock photo; **p.52** © Sergey Nivens/stock.adobe.com; **p.56** © Jale Ibrak/stock.adobe.com; **p.57** *m* © Karpenko_ilia/stock.adobe.com; *b* © Sidop/stock.adobe.com; **p.58** © Syda Productions/stock.adobe.com; **p.59** © pressmaster – Fotolia; **p.62** *t* © ra2 studio/stock.adobe.com; *b* © Martin/stock.adobe.com; **p.63** © Mejn/stock.adobe.com; **p.64** © Mediteraneo/stock.adobe.com; **p.70** © Rawpixel.com/stock.adobe.com; **p.73** © Monkey Business/stock.adobe.com; **p.74** © Tostphoto/stock.adobe.com; **p.78** © Fizkes/stock.adobe.com; **p.80** © Rawpixel.com/stock.adobe.com; **p.81** © rms164/stock.adobe.com; **p.82** © John Stanmeyer/National Geographic Creative; **p.83** © 5second/stock.adobe.com; **p.88** © Kieferpix/stock.adobe.com; **p.90** © International Baccalaureate Organization 2019; **p.95** © Egokhan/stock.adobe.com; **p.96** © Egokhan/stock.adobe.com; **p.97** © Monster Ztudio/stock.adobe.com; **p.100** © Karen Roach/stock.adobe.com; **p.101** © Pixsooz/stock.adobe.com; **p.102** © Visions-AD/stock.adobe.com; **p.105** © Tinatin/stock.adobe.com; **p.107** © Jacob Lund/stock.adobe.com; **p.111** © Aaron Amat/stock.adobe.com

Text credits:

p.25 Nur YelizGülcan, (2015). 'Discussing the Importance of Teaching Ethics in Education'. *Procedia - Social and Behavioral Sciences.* Volume 174, 12 February 2015, Pages 2622–2625.**https://doi.org/10.1016/j.sbspro.2015.01.942**; **p.26** Common Ethical Issues from *Principles of biomedical ethics* by Tom L. Beauchamp and James F. Childress. Oxford Publishing Limited 1958. Reproduced with permission of the Licensor through PLSclear; **p.34** My Own Words Quotes by Ruth Bader Ginsburg; **p.34** Reproduced by kind permission of the Estate of Martha Gellhorn; **p.34** 'There is nothing radical about moral clarity in 2018.' Alexandria Ocasio-Cortez; **p.35** Quote 'I am a thinker, and I do muse over things a lot and am constantly assessing whether I am doing enough or what I should be doing more of to make sure I am not letting anyone down.' by Jacinda Ardern; **p.35** Barack Obama (2007). 'The Audacity of Hope: Thoughts on Reclaiming the American Dream', p.68, Canongate Books; **p.46** From: Joseph Fletcher, 'Naturalism, situation ethics and value theory', in Ethics at the Crossroads, 1995; **p.46** From Peter Vardy and Paul Grosch, 'The Puzzle of Ethics' (1994).